Bay of Pigs

Dedicated to Riley Shamburger,
Pete Ray, Leo Baker and Wade Gray

Bay of Pigs

*A Firsthand Account of
the Mission by a U.S. Pilot
in Support of the Cuban
Invasion Force in 1961*

by
Albert C. Persons

with a foreword by
JOSEPH L. SHANNON

McFarland & Company, Inc., Publishers
Jefferson, North Carolina, and London

British Library Cataloguing-in-Publication data are available

Library of Congress Cataloguing-in-Publication Data

Persons, Albert C., 1915–
Bay of Pigs : a firsthand account of the mission by a U.S. pilot
in support of the Cuban invasion force in 1961
/ by Albert C. Persons.
p.   cm.
[Includes index.]
Includes bibliographical references.
ISBN 0-89950-483-3 (sewn softcover : 50# alk. paper) ∞
1. Cuba – History – Invasion, 1961 – Personal narratives.
2. Cuba – History – Invasion, 1961 – Aerial operations.
3. United States. Central Intelligence Agency.
4. Persons, Albert C., 1915–   .
I. Title.
F1788.P47   1990
972.9106′4 – dc20
89-13566
CIP

Manufactured in the United States of America

McFarland & Company, Inc., Publishers
Box 611, Jefferson, North Carolina 28640

Contents

DA

Foreword

Buck Persons' memoir reflects the personal experiences of a group of pilots hired by the CIA to fly support missions for the Cuban invasion force which landed at the Bay of Pigs in 1961. Unlike other accounts of the Bay of Pigs, most written by professional journalists, *Bay of Pigs: A Firsthand Account* leaves little doubt that the failure of that mission did not originate at the Central American air bases from which the attack was launched. Nor was it due to flaws in the operational plan as it was conceived, but rather to unanticipated, last-minute, nonmilitary restrictions of that plan. It is revealing that what Buck describes from firsthand observation bears so little resemblance to official postmortems as prepared in Washington.

It appears that no one responsible for the planning and operation of the assault knew how to execute an attack on a beach. For example, it was absurd to launch air strikes against Castro's air bases two full days before the D-day assault; the timing of those attacks gave Castro ample warning that the invasion he had been expecting for months was imminent. But in 1961 the command structure of our intelligence and defense establishment included experts in this area, veterans of beach landings throughout the Pacific in World War II. This expertise was utilized both in initial planning and in the field with us. However, these experts had no intention of leaving two-thirds of our air strike force on the ground when air attacks were launched against Castro's air bases on Saturday.

Riley Shamburger was my wingman in an attack on targets on the beach east of Giron on Wednesday morning. I saw him crash into the sea after being shot down by one of Castro's two remaining armed jet trainers. This is not to say that some of us supporting the effort to remove Castro from power may not have lost our lives in any event, but we should not have had to face unnecessary risks. The Lockheed T-33 that killed Riley and Wade Gray should not even have been in the air on that morning.

Riley and I were attached as "training advisors" to the Cuban exiles' "Liberation Air Force," so I got to know the Cuban pilots much better than Buck did. He spent most of his time flying C-54 cargo aircraft between our bases in Guatemala and Nicaragua. The Cuban pilots were a courageous and dedicated group. They may not have had all the information they would have liked to have had, but in "special activities" like these no one ever has any more information than is essential to the performance of his specific job. We were never able to convince the Cubans that all of the Americans, including Riley and me, did not know everything there was to know, and that we were not "holding out" on them. But in truth we did not know any more than was necessary for us to carry out our own assignments.

When Buck saw the "consternation" on the faces of our people in the operations center, he had no way of knowing that the "long line" from Washington was carrying orders which progressively reduced our chances of success. Nor could he have known that when Castro's few surviving aircraft sank the *Houston* and the *Rio Escondido* on Monday morning that those ships were lost with all of the Brigade's communications equipment and ammunition resupply, resources essential to the success of the operation. Moreover, Buck could not have known that available intelligence indicated that Castro may have been down to his last gallon of fuel, and that his ordnance was nearly exhausted when the battle ended on Wednesday afternoon. Execution of the operation as originally planned, with full employment of our resources in a determined effort, could have meant the difference between a military victory and humiliating failure.

Through the months of organization and training in Central America, no doubt there were rumors and speculation among the Cubans about how much and what kind of support they could expect from the U.S. government. With enough repetition, some of these rumors may have naturally taken on substance as "straight poop." In any case, the Cubans had absolute faith in the intentions and abilities of the United States government in whose hands they placed their destiny. There was never any reason for the Cubans to have anticipated the fiasco that actually occurred. Understandably, most of the Cubans still feel a certain amount of bitterness, that they were let down, even abandoned on the beaches at the Bay of Pigs.

This book is the story of one man's personal observations and assessments. Its greatest value may be that it is unencumbered by any effort to encompass all possible sources of comment, glaring errors and preconceived conclusions characteristic of other supposedly definitive works. What Buck Persons describes is based on what he observed as an actual participant, and on the discrepancies between his observations and officially authorized accounts of the doomed operation. In my opinion the conclusions Buck draws, based on his own experiences, are well founded and make an historical contribution to a controversial event.

Joseph L. Shannon (Hal McGee)
Lieutenant Colonel, USAF (ret.)

Preface

The last half of the 20th century will no doubt be viewed by historians as a period in which the two most powerful nations on earth engaged in a continuing contest for preeminence and for the power to influence and guide the evolution of political ideologies throughout the world for generations to come. In this struggle, enormous allotments of the national patrimony of each side were washed away, with what impact on the future political and social histories of the two nations, historians themselves will judge.

In April 1961 the failure to remove Fidel Castro from power in Cuba was a setback in efforts by the United States to prevent the spread of Soviet influence over less powerful nations, particularly in our own hemisphere. The episode at the Bay of Pigs on Cuba's south coast was an unsuccessful invasion attempt by an armed force of exile Cubans which had been organized, supplied and trained by the United States government. Whether the failure of this effort will be seen as an historically major event, or insignificant, only time and the course of future events will tell.

For the most part, the theme of investigative journalists and other chroniclers who have written about the Bay of Pigs has been that the president of the United States was the victim of inexcusably bad advice; that he should never have permitted one agency of government to conceive and execute its own plans without review by other more objective authority; that nothing really went wrong that could have been prevented, and that every possible effort was made that could have been made to carry out a mission that was fatally flawed from the start. This is the raw material from which historians will fashion their own views and assessments of the event. Based on my own observations as an eye witness and as a participant in the failed mission at the Bay of Pigs, this material is seriously flawed.

One of the troubles with history is that so much of it is written by people whose knowledge is limited to what other people have written or said. Human nature being what it is, causal conclusions that are free of value and or moral judgments probably should not be expected. And the farther in time we become removed from the historical event, the more it becomes necessary to accept accounts that may be based on information that is false, self-serving or, unknown to us, may be too thoroughly value-impregnated by the chroniclers themselves.

The current event, of course, is not history. The current event is "news." It becomes history in some future period in time when it is possible to view the event in total perspective, to link it accurately with events that preceded it, and to assess its impact on events that followed. Had Leonidas and 300 Spartans, for instance, not held the Persian army off at the pass at Thermopylae, Greek and Roman civilizations might not have survived to make their contributions to the culture of the western world. If Charles Martel had not stopped the Muslim hordes on the plain at Tours, we might all be worshipping in mosques today instead of cathedrals. And if William of Normandy had not defeated King Harold, Magna Carta might never have been born. To write history accurately, of course, the sources of information must be as factual as reliable records permit. To even speak of history as being "accurate" or "inaccurate" may be a contradiction in terms. If it is not accurate, it is not history, it is something else — like fiction.

What happened at Thermopylae doesn't matter much today — nor Tours, nor Hastings. And it is unlikely that in 2,400 years (or even 240 years) there will be more than a footnote mention of the Bay of Pigs. However, it might have been different. If the Cuban missile crisis in 1962 had gone the other way, for instance, with a nuclear holocaust as a result, our failure in 1961 to remove a Soviet garrison from an island only 90 miles off our own shores would have assumed far greater historical importance.

No doubt there is more to the Bay of Pigs episode than what is described here. But if there is anything of value to be learned from history, and historians insist that there is, then this memoir should give historians, and anyone else who is interested, something quite different to look at and consider, for the Bay of Pigs has a peculiar and lingering flavor all its own. Like wild onions in the front yard, it seems destined to keep cropping up.

Maps

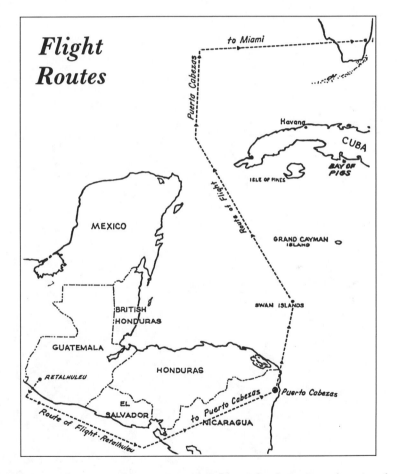

Flight Routes

The maps on this page and page xii provide reference for the various places involved in the narrative of Bay of Pigs. On page xiii, the map explains the Trinidad Plan which was abandoned in favor of the Bay of Pigs site.

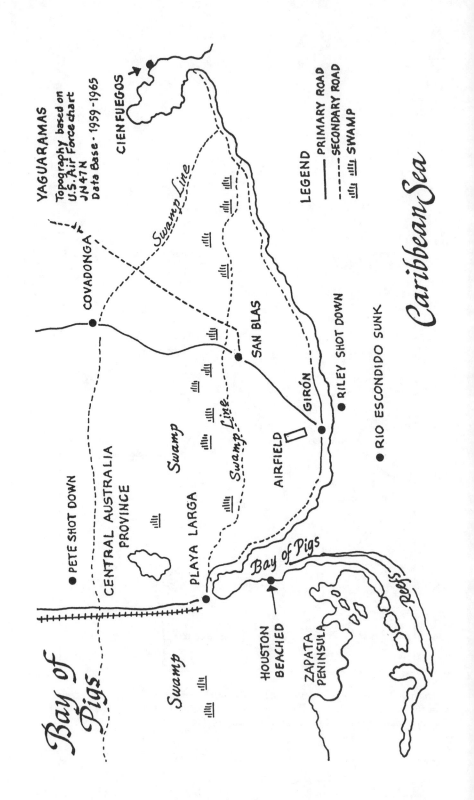

Bay of Pigs

YAGUARAMAS

Topography based on
U.S. Air Force chart
JN47N
Data Base · 1959-1965

CIEN FUEGOS

COVADONGA

Swamp Line

SAN BLAS

GIRÓN

RILEY SHOT DOWN

RIO ESCONDIDO SUNK

LEGEND
—— PRIMARY ROAD
---- SECONDARY ROAD
� SWAMP

PETE SHOT DOWN

CENTRAL AUSTRALIA
PROVINCE

Swamp

PLAYA LARGA

Swamp Line

AIRFIELD

Swamp

Bay of Pigs

HOUSTON
BEACHED

ZAPATA
PENINSULA

Reefs

Caribbean Sea

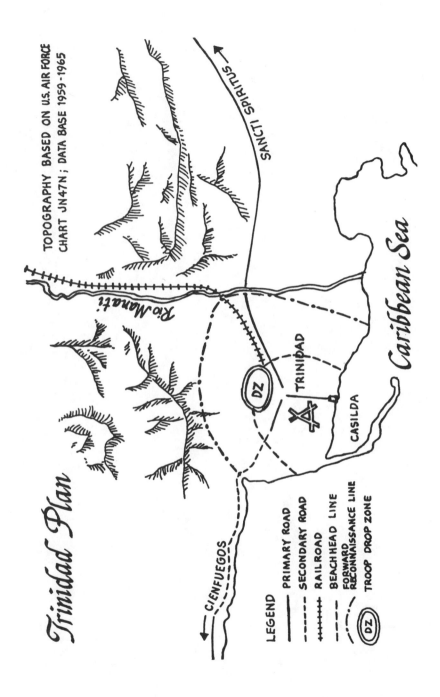

Trinidad Plan

TOPOGRAPHY BASED ON U.S. AIR FORCE
CHART JN47N; DATA BASE 1959-1965

SANCTI SPIRITUS

Rio Manati

CIENFUEGOS

DZ

TRINIDAD

CASILDA

Caribbean Sea

LEGEND

———————— PRIMARY ROAD
—·—·—·—·— SECONDARY ROAD
—+—+—+—+— RAILROAD
———————— BEACHHEAD LINE
—··—··—··— FORWARD
          RECONNAISSANCE LINE
(DZ)   TROOP DROP ZONE

Mission to Zapata

Pete Ray checked his watch. There was a hint on the horizon that the long night was ending. He reached forward to the throttles, reduced power on the B-26's two R-2800s, and began a slow descent from 8,000 feet, holding the airspeed at 250 knots.

As the early morning light increased, the fluorescent glow on the instrument panels dimmed. The throttle quadrant, radios, and flight and engine instruments began to take shape in the cockpit. Finally, the face of the sea emerged from the darkness, rushing aft only 150 feet below the wings of the aircraft.

Pete was in the left seat behind the control column of the B-26. His throat was beginning to feel sore from too many cigarettes chain-smoked through the night. His T-shirt, soaked with sweat earlier, was cold and damp against his skin, and in the close confines of the cockpit, Pete was aware of his own body odor. Low in his bowels he began to feel the apprehension that precedes combat.

In the observer's seat beside Pete, Leo Baker stirred and swallowed hard a couple of times to relieve the pressure on his ears. Leo's eyes were fixed on the horizon. The clean, sharp line began to blur, then became uneven and broken. The south coast of Cuba rose slowly out of the sea twenty miles ahead. Neither man spoke. In fact, Pete and Leo had not exchanged a word since takeoff two and a half hours earlier from Puerto Cabezas on Nicaragua's gulf coast.

The men on shore heard the roar of engines overhead as the B-26 came in at treetop level off the Bay of Pigs and disappeared over the inland swamps. The remnants of a Cuban invasion force that had come ashore two days earlier were barely hanging on to a rapidly shrinking beachhead. A paved airstrip at Girón was still in their hands, but not for long. A C-46 from the base at Puerto Cabezas landed later that morning with a load of medical supplies and communications equipment. When it took off for the return trip to Nicaragua, Castro's armored columns were already pushing into the area on three access roads from the north, northeast and east. In the operational plan the airstrip at Girón was to have been used for air

1

resupply of the invasion force after the beachhead had been secured. The C-46 was the only aircraft to land on the beach during the three-day battle at the Bay of Pigs.

The Bay of Pigs is surrounded by nearly impenetrable swamps. From the air the Zapata swamps showed dense and green through the patches of heavy ground fog that blanketed the coastal area. Through a break in the fog Leo caught sight of a thin ribbon of dirt road angling off to the right of the aircraft's course. He nudged Pete, who nodded without turning his head. The aircraft banked steeply, leveled off and flew inland, following the road toward a column of black, oily smoke that rose perpendicular from the ground a few miles ahead. Twenty minutes later Pete picked up the microphone in the cockpit, pressed the key, and in a tight, even voice said, "We're going in."

Evidence at the time indicated that Pete and Leo were shot down by ground fire from militia troops stationed in the area of a sugar plantation in Central Australia Province just north of the Bay of Pigs. Their B-26 crashed in an open field. Pictures smuggled out of Cuba later showed that the aircraft suffered heavy damage, but was not completely destroyed. Witnesses said that Leo survived the crash and came out of the cockpit with his .45 automatic in his hand. He was immediately shot down. If Pete survived the crash, he was badly injured. A photograph of both men lying on the ground beside the aircraft eventually showed up in the States.

Hal McGee, flying just ahead of Riley Shamburger on a strafing run along the beach, heard Riley come on the air with the words, "Hit! Hit!" Hal made a swift, steep turn just as a T-Bird flashed past his wing. The T-Bird was one of two remaining Lockheed jet trainers Castro had converted to fighters. Hal saw Riley and his observer, Wade Gray, crash in flames in the water off shore.

Four other B-26s returned to the base at Puerto Cabezas later that morning. Don Gordon was escorted off the beach by three unmarked U.S. Navy jet fighters. The fighters flew in formation with the B-26 until Don signalled the pilots to break off and return to their patrol of the beach.

Months later in Washington, it was explained that the Navy air combat patrol over the beaches at the Bay of Pigs had been ineffective because a "mix-up" in timing had put the Navy fighters in and out of the area before the invasion force B-26s arrived. The U.S. Navy air combat patrol may not have been effective, but not because of any "mix-up" in timing. The Navy jets were there at the time they were supposed to have been.

The day was Wednesday, April 19, 1961. By nightfall, the last echoes of the three-day battle at the Bay of Pigs had died.

Late that afternoon, six hundred miles across the Gulf of Mexico, a Catholic priest walked out from Puerto Cabezas to our tent camp pitched close by the end of a 5,000-foot paved runway. The priest arrived in camp just before dark to perform a funeral mass for Leo. He erected an altar from ammunition boxes and empty crates. The makeshift altar was protected from the first heavy drops of an afternoon thunder shower by a canvas tarpaulin strung from the lower branches of surrounding trees. The priest was assisted in the mass by a Cuban dressed in a dirty T-shirt, shorts, and unlaced hunting boots. Quietly in the darkness the men began to gather. Those who were Catholic knelt with heads bowed. Candle flames flickered and bent flat before the wind. Night sounds from the jungle close by accompanied the priest as he performed the ritual service. I have never talked to anyone who could tell me how that priest knew that Leo Baker had lost his life that morning, and how he knew that Leo was Catholic. A small detachment of Nicaraguan Air Force personnel, with one P-51 "Mustang" fighter, occupied facilities at the end of the field. They must have known in a general sort of way what we were up to, but I would not think they would have been privy to anything as specific as the circumstances of the loss of Pete and Leo. It was, and remains, an unsolved and intriguing mystery.

When the funeral service was over, I walked back to the tent where Leo and I lived. There were a few articles of clothing hanging from nails in the tent pole beside Leo's cot. I folded these and a thin army blanket and put them into a blue canvas duffle bag. There were two letters under the pillow and a pair of sandals under the cot. I put these into the duffle bag and pulled the drawstring tight.

Five men were gathered at the far end of the tent drinking beer. They were huddled together on two cots away from the gusts of rain that blew in under the walls of the tent. A naked light bulb hung from the ridge pole over their heads. I tossed Leo's duffle bag onto his cot and joined the other men. One of them dug into a small ice chest and handed me a cold beer.

"Goddamnit to hell," he said.

"What the hell *happened*?" another man said.

What *happened* was that a United States government–planned military operation to remove Fidel Castro from power in Cuba had failed.

Birmingham

In the early part of January, 1961, I became involved in the affair that cost Riley Shamburger, Pete Ray, Leo Baker and Wade Gray their lives at the Bay of Pigs. At the time, I was flying a DC-3 for Harbert International, a Birmingham construction company. I was what is known in the trade as a "corporate pilot," a professional pilot employed to fly aircraft owned by a private company.

In addition to the DC-3, Harbert owned two other aircraft, a single engine Bonanza and a twin-engine Cessna 310. We stored all three aircraft at the municipal airport. There were two other pilots on the payroll, Ed Friday and Les Cruse. Ed was assigned primarily to the Bonanza, but he flew with me on occasion in the DC-3. Les, who was a skilled mechanic as well as a pilot, flew with me on the DC-3, and he was responsible for maintenance and periodic inspections on all three aircraft.

Harbert had contracts all over the country, and the three of us were "on the road" most of the time. This probably accounts for the fact that I was unaware of all the rumors that had been circulating around the airport for some time, rumors involving the Air Guard unit stationed at Birmingham, and a mysterious and secret mission somewhere out of the country.

I arrived at the hangar about noon one day in the first week in January. Ed and I were supposed to help Les run an inspection on the DC-3. I found Ed in a state of unsuppressed excitement. He said that Riley Shamburger had been trying to get in touch with me all morning. I asked Ed if he knew why Riley wanted to see me. He said that Riley was "lining up" people for a flying job, one that required considerable flying experience and a military background.

"I've already got a job," I said, "or at least I did when I left the office about an hour ago."

"No, no. This isn't a permanent job. This is a temporary, confidential deal. You'll have to get leave, or something. You'd better get on over to Hayes and see Riley. And listen! See if you can fix me up, too. I want to go with you guys."

"Friday! What is this all about?"

"Cap'n Buck, they're going to start a revolution! Where do you think all those Guard guys have been going?"

"I didn't know they'd been going anywhere. What Guard guys are you talking about? Where's the revolution?"

"Buck, there isn't hardly a ground crew left over there." Ed waved toward the north side of the airport where the Alabama Air Guard facilities were located. "They've been going out for the last two or three weeks. They're going to invade *Cuba*. That's why Riley is lining up C-54 pilots. I don't know where they've all been going, but it's supposed to be somewhere in Central America — maybe Venezuela." (Geography was not Ed's long suit.)

I hadn't heard any of these stories. I knew Major General Reid Doster and a few of the pilots in the 117th Tactical Reconnaissance Wing, the Alabama Air Guard unit commanded by Doster. I had no Air Guard connections myself, however, and I knew very few of the ground support people in the unit. Friday had done a year's tour of duty with the 117th Wing after graduating from flying school. He ran around with several of the younger Guard pilots. From them he had learned that many of the enlisted specialists had been leaving Birmingham at intervals, and that they were supposed to be "somewhere down in Central America."

Urged on by Ed, who was practically snapping at my heels, I drove around the field to the Hayes Aircraft hangars. Hayes was an aircraft modification center in Birmingham working almost exclusively on Air Force contracts. Riley Shamburger was a test pilot for Hayes. He was also a Major and a squadron operations officer in the Air Guard. I found Riley at the Hayes flight test operations building.

"Friday says you're looking for me, Riley. What's up?"

"How much four-engine time you got, Buck?"

"I don't know. About twelve hundred hours on B-17s and a hundred or so on 24s."

"I'm working on a deal with Reid," Riley said. "We need some four-engine drivers with military experience. It's out of this country. I can't tell you where at the moment. All I can tell you is that it's legitimate and shouldn't last more than a couple of months if you can get leave from Harbert. Can you work that out?"

"I guess I *could* if it's important enough," I said. "You say this job is 'legitimate.' Are you under some impression that what I'm doing now is *not* legitimate?"

"Oh bullshit, Buck. Listen, this *is* important. Reid is out of town until next week. How about talking to him when he get's back."

"Okay, I'll talk to him. Meantime, how about giving me some kind of clue. I can't just walk down to the office and *quit*."

"Like I said, I can't. But I know you'll buy it. Are you scheduled to go out?"

"I've got a trip to Oke City Monday. I'll be back in Wednesday."

"I'll tell Reid you'll call him when you get back?"

"Sure. I'll call him. Meanwhile Riley, when does this so-called legitimate job get started?"

"Right away. The next couple of weeks."

"That's great. I'll have time to get some laundry done. By the way, what kind of clothes will I be needing where we're going?"

"You won't need any clothes. We're all going to be running around naked. Just call Reid, Buck. And I guess you know this is all kind of confidential."

"It sure as hell is so far."

"Okay. Just keep it under your hat—if you own one."

This was the first knowledge I had of an operation like the one Riley suggested was in the making. It made a certain amount of sense. What all the rumors may have lacked in accurate detail, in substance were probably well founded. Three months earlier while in San Diego, I read a newspaper story about an American contractor who was building an airstrip in Guatemala—an extremely hush-hush job under tight security controls. Now, I believed, I had a clue to suggest where all the Air Guard troops from across the field may have been headed when they "disappeared."

On Wednesday in the week following my conversation with Riley, I returned from a flight to Oklahoma City. Twenty miles out of Birmingham I called the control tower for landing instructions.

"Runway two-three, twenty-two-how-charlie, winds light and variable, altimeter two niner niner eight, report Roebuck."

I reported on final over Roebuck Shopping Center and was cleared to land. It was late in the afternoon of a gray, overcast day. The shopping center parking lot was full. Lights blazed in all the stores. Street lights were beginning to come on. I touched down on the runway and Les raised the flaps and unlocked the tail wheel. When we turned off the runway, ground control cleared us all the way to the ramp. A minute later ground control called back, "General Doster requests Buck Persons to come to his office when he gets the airplane parked."

The 117th Tactical Reconnaissance Wing of the Alabama Air Guard is located on the north side of Birmingham's municipal airport. It was dark as I drove around the field and parked beside the two-story headquarters building. Colonel Burt Gurley was in his office next to General Doster's.

"Come on in, Buck. The General's waiting for you."

Burt preceded me into the General's office, then backed out, closing the door behind him. I shook hands with Doster, then sat down in a chair beside his desk.

"What's it all about, Reid?"

"Buck, I've got a job to recruit six experienced pilots for four-engine work, and six B-26 pilots. These have to be pilots with previous military experience, but with no current military connections. I want you for C-54s. About all I can tell you about the job right now is this. It's outside the continental limits of the United States. It's in this hemisphere. There may be some shooting involved, and it's very much in the interest of our government. The job will last about three months."

"When does all this get started?"

"You'll be leaving in about two or three weeks — if you want to go. If you do, I need to know now, tonight. I've got my B-26 pilots lined up and I've been waiting for you to get back to fill out the C-54 crews. I'll need to get your clearance tonight if you're going to go."

"That sounds like I've got to give you a yes or no answer right now, sitting right here."

"It's not much notice. You might say none at all, but time is running out and I took a chance on counting on you."

"Well, what the hell. In that case, go ahead and put me down to go."

"All right. Be back over here Monday morning at eight o'clock. Some people will be down from Washington for a briefing. Now don't say anything about this at home for the time being. There'll be some instructions on how to clear yourself with your family on this thing, and I don't want any of you pilots jumping the gun. The same thing goes for your jobs. Everybody's getting a leave of absence, including me, or otherwise working their job problems out. But don't try to do anything until after you've been briefed Monday morning. Are you going to have any problems?"

"No," I said, "I don't think I'll have any problems." There were questions, but this didn't seem like the time to ask them. "So, I'll see you Monday."

"Okay, Buck. I'm sorry I can't go into any more detail right now. You can figure anything out you want to for yourself — and I guess you'll be pretty close."

The things I could figure out for myself were pretty obvious. General Doster would not have had any part of an operation that involved aircraft and "shooting" if it were not something that the United States government was directly involved in. It was also obvious that it was a covert operation, or there would have been no reason to recruit people like me. All of this spelled only one thing — Cuba, with whom we had severed diplomatic relations 15 months after Fidel Castro came to power.

General Doster stopped me as I walked toward the door. "Hey!"

I looked back.

"Don't you want to know how much the job pays?"

"Well — I don't know whether I do or not. How much?"

"Twenty-eight hundred dollars a month with some bonus arrangements."

"That ought to tell me something, I guess." (Twenty-eight hundred dollars in 1961 was equivalent to six thousand 1987 dollars.)

"Yes, I guess it ought to," Doster said, "see ya."

On the way home I thought about the "bonus arrangements." Bonuses are paid for something over and above the duties normally called for by a job. In this case, it seemed that any bonuses would be tied in closely to the "shooting" Reid had mentioned.

In my mind, there was little doubt that the United States viewed Castro and his regime, and his connections with international communism, with alarm. At the highest levels in government, it must have been decided that the security of the United States was in danger as long as Castro remained in power, and a decision had been made to do something about it. Through what channels all this got bucked down the line to General Doster was a matter of pure speculation. In any case, I had apparently been invited to help out — at least that is the way I chose to look at it.

General Doster had said something about having to get me cleared that night. The briefing by the people from Washington was only four days off. How could anyone with no military or government connections for more than twenty years be cleared for an operation like this in a matter of hours? Any records of mine were bound to be buried ten feet deep in some warehouse. I was in General Doster's office the next morning before nine o'clock.

"Reid, last night you said that you would have to get me cleared immediately for this job. The briefing is Monday morning. I don't see any way I can get cleared in this length of time. I haven't had any military service since World War II. . . ."

"Hold it, hold it," Reid interrupted, "You're all cleared. Just be here Monday morning."

"You mean since last night . . . that doesn't seem . . . is that definite?"

"Not necessarily since last night, as you put it, but it's definite. Just be here Monday."

On the way out of the headquarters building I met Hal McGee. Hal was a Colonel in the 117th Wing. I had known him casually for several years.

"Are you all set, Buck?" Hal asked.

"I guess so," I answered cautiously. "How about you?"

"Riley and I, and the General, have to go to Washington this afternoon. We may not be back until late Sunday night. I just wanted to be sure that you are lined up for the briefing Monday."

I hadn't known of Hal's involvement but, then, until a few days before I hadn't known anything, much less who might be involved. I learned from

Hal that General Doster had had some difficulty finding pilots who were without current military connections, but had the desired background and experience. When the pilots arrived in Birmingham for the briefing, they came in from many sections of the country.

On Monday morning I reported at Air Guard Headquarters at eight o'clock. Hal McGee was in the hall outside General Doster's office.

"Where's the briefing, Hal?"

"Go upstairs and down to the far end of the hall on the other end of the building. There's a bunch of the guys already there."

"Are you coming?"

"No, I won't be in on the briefing," Hal said. "I've already been briefed. So has Riley. We're part of the program, but we have a little bit different deal."

Riley and Hal were on a somewhat higher plane than the rest of us. In fact, as I learned later, both were even "higher briefed" than General Doster. All three had been involved in some phases of the mission planning. They knew considerably more about the operation than our group of airmen did — which, at the moment, was nothing. Because of their levels of prior participation, it was never contemplated that Hal or Riley would be expected, or permitted, to do any combat flying.

In the hall upstairs a group of men were gathered around a coffee urn on a table against the wall. I met Bill Peterson, Al Walters, Joe Hinkle, and Pete Ray who were B-26 pilots. Pete lived in a small town close to Birmingham. The others were from out of state. Ernie King and Gordon Neilson were C-54 pilots. They had known each other in the Korean War. Sandy Sanders had been a flight engineer and crew chief with the Guard unit in Birmingham. Red Cornish was another flight engineer who had known Riley somewhere. There were several other men in the group who were not immediately identifiable.

I shook hands with several of the pilots. We exchanged a few noncommital remarks. No one had known who, or how many, would be in the group. No one knew what the process of selection had been. There was a certain amount of suppressed curiosity as we all milled around trying to act as if we knew what we were doing. Everyone was speculating about how much the other guys knew that he didn't know. Joe Hinkle walked over to where I was standing by the coffee pot.

"Buck, I see you've been elected. What are you going to fly?"

"C-54s according to Reid. What about you?"

"I'm on B-26s. The best I can figure out we've got two sets of pilots. Bill Peterson, Al Walters, Ron Smith, Don Gordon and I are all B-26 drivers. That guy over there, I think his name is Ealey, he's a C-54 pilot. I don't know where he's from. I don't know the other people, but I guess they must be part of the C-54 crews."

Ernie King walked up while Joe was talking. "That's Wade Gray," he said, pointing to a man with curly, prematurely gray hair, and the guy beside him is Jack Vernon. They're both radio operators."

"What are we going to do with radio operators?" I asked. "I haven't had a radio operator on an airplane since World War II."

"I don't know," Joe said, "but it looks to me as if we must be going way out in the boondocks somewhere."

"What's the hold up now?" I asked Joe.

"We're waiting for Ron to get in with a guy from Tampa. He left about six this morning in a T-Bird to pick him up. They should be getting in any minute now."

Ron arrived ten minutes later with a man he introduced as Earl Carter. Leo Baker also showed up. I knew Leo. He was a flight engineer for Hayes. Reid Doster came up the stairs and told everyone to go down to the end of the hall to the conference room. There was one long table in the room. Four men were sitting at the table when we entered, one at the head, the other three beside him along one side. I sat down next to the man at the head of the table and directly across from the other three. One of the men got up and shut the door. When we were all seated, the man at the head of the table said, "Gentlemen, I'm Al." Al introduced the other three men as "Frank," "Jake" and "Hoyt."

This was our initiation into the never-never land of covert operations in which people were always emerging briefly from, and disappearing back into, a misty atmosphere that enshrouded all activity and reduced visibility to almost zero. Ideally, no one tried to look much farther than where his next step would take him. People knew and addressed one another by first names only. They had last names, but they were phony. In fact, these last names were referred to among themselves as their "phonies." The phonies were always supported by equally bogus documentation — a phony drivers license, a phony Social Security card, birth certificate, etc. The more permanent residents of this covert world changed phonies the way they changed clothes, to suit the climate and the circumstances of the moment.

In due time we were all relabeled with our own phonies and accompanying documentation. Since our phonies were not designed to disguise our identities from each other, but only, in certain emergencies, from members of the real world, we never committed to memory other people's phonies. In fact, we were sometimes hard put to remember our own.

Al's story was that he and the other three men were agents for a group of wealthy Cubans who were financing an operation to overthrow Fidel Castro. He said that with General Doster's help we had been recruited to perform combat missions that were vital to the success of this effort. Al said that they already had the necessary aircraft and, in fact, they even had aircrews whom he described as "foreign nationals."

It seems that Al and his group did not feel entirely confident that these "foreign nationals" would be able to perform successfully when the time came to launch the first strikes against Castro. They were pilots of varying degrees of experience. They were brave and dedicated, but without combat experience. Some were quite low on flying time, particularly in high performance aircraft. Therefore, Al and his people felt that it was necessary to recruit pilots who had previous combat experience and who could be counted on to carry out missions against military targets, and to press home other assignments that would precede assaults by ground forces.

As Al talked, I studied him and the three men who sat across the table from me. Al was pleasant and articulate. He was a man in his mid-forties. He had black hair and a toothbrush mustache. He looked a lot like Melvin Douglas, the movie actor, and his manner was more that of a sales manager conducting a seminar than of a person conspiring to overthrow the head of a government.

We were to see a lot more of Al in the weeks to come in Central America. He and one of the men with him, Frank, were top commanders in the field.

Hollywood would never have cast Frank in his role. Frank would have been in character as, say, a bookkeeper or a ladies shoe salesman, never as a tough, competent director of covert military operations. If you had to scan a crowd for a guy who looked as if he might have a gun holstered under his jacket (and he knew how to use it), you would pass right over Frank without a second glance. He was about five feet, five inches tall and, as they say, couldn't have weighed more than 135 pounds soaking wet. His hair was a nondescript brown, thin and wispy. There was one thing in particular that I noticed about Frank however. He had bright, intelligent eyes that swept constantly and pleasantly from face to face around the table as we talked. Jake and Hoyt, on the other hand, were grim and expressionless. I remember thinking, "Here are a couple of guys you could never make friends with."

Jake was very tall and very thin, with the prominent Adam's apple that often goes with that build. Hoyt was of medium height, medium weight, medium build, completely medium all the way — neutral. If he robbed your bank, you would never be able to describe him to the cops. Because of the contrast in their physical appearances, they were not like two peas in a pod, but you knew they had to have come off the same bush. When one of the men around the table spoke, their stony eyes moved in his direction and remained fixed on the speaker until he had finished. It was apparent that they had been through this drill many times before, and were not edified by anything anyone had to say. Jake and Hoyt were not people that I could imagine with wives and kiddies somewhere; with garbage to take out, lawns to mow and cars to wash on Sunday afternoon. On the other hand,

I could have been 100 percent wrong. Just because you don't sell shoes or insurance for a living, or keep books, or work for the gas company, doesn't mean that you don't have kids and garbage and a car that needs washing on Sunday afternoon — if you happen to be anywhere in the neighborhood, that is. We saw Jake and Hoyt only once again. That was at a second briefing ten days later in the same conference room where their roles, if not their identities, came into somewhat sharper focus.

Al described in somewhat skimpy detail what our jobs would be. Like General Doster, he would only say that we would be based outside the continental limits of the United States, but in this hemisphere. No mention of a country, or countries. The C-54 pilots would drop equipment and troops after hostilities began. Beforehand, they would do a lot of flying to transport people, equipment and supplies between various bases. Al said that on occasion we might have to fly with some of the "foreign nationals" (for some reason he refused to identify them as Cubans), but he said that in any such event, we would always be in command of the aircraft. Al said that the B-26 pilots would have some training responsibilities and would be expected to perform the first critical bombing and strafing missions.

Finally, Al instructed everyone to prepare a "cover story" to explain our absence from home and jobs. These stories would have to be well thought out and convincing. He didn't care what they were. Each of us would know best what would be convincing wherever convincing was required. We were instructed to prepare these cover stories before the next, and final, briefing, and to be prepared to check them out with Al and his three associates whose trained eyes could be counted on to detect any serious structural flaws.

Each of us was also asked to come up with the name of a city, anywhere in the United States, with which we were sufficiently familiar to know the names of some streets and places. These had to be large cities, not small towns. Then he asked if anyone had any questions. At this point I detected the first signs of life in the two stone faces of Jake and Hoyt.

I had one question: "It is clear that this is a military operation," I said, "and you have mentioned the foreign nationals and the fact that we might have to fly with them on occasion. You have also mentioned your employers, the group of wealthy Cubans. What I want to ask is this: Is it safe to assume that the military aspects of this operation will be under the control of, say, professional military people, rather than under the control of the foreign nationals and the wealthy Cubans?"

"You can be sure," Al replied, "that this operation is being planned and conducted by professionals in whom you can place complete confidence. You will take your orders from us. As I said previously, if you have any occasion to fly with foreign aircrews, none of them will ever be in command of the aircraft."

Ron Smith wanted to know if we would "have to shoot any civilians."

Al replied that all of the targets would be military targets, a reasonably ambiguous answer. I noticed that the eyes in the two stone faces lingered for an extra second or two on Ron.

The only other questions were asked by two men at the end of the table. They probed for more details, which was a mistake. Neither of them was present at the second briefing.

It was apparent that there would be no discussion of specifics. As for Al's story about the "wealthy Cubans," the fact that we were being briefed at the headquarters of the 117th Tactical Reconnaissance Wing of the Alabama Air Guard made it quite clear that wealthy Cuban exiles were neither the architects nor the source of financing for the planned overthrow of the Castro government in Cuba.

Ten days later our group (minus the two inquisitors at the end of the table) met once more at the Air Guard headquarters. This time there was no roundtable discussion. There was no more talk about wealthy Cuban exiles either. We were told that we were now working for an electronics company in New England. Al didn't bother to explain what had happened to the original story, but he clearly expected us to have no difficulty making the transition from one story to the other.

At the second briefing we went one at a time into separate offices where we talked first to Jake, then to Hoyt. Jake went over our cover stories with us. No one had shown much imagination. We had all invented opportunities to attend specialized training courses in new fields of aviation or electronics.

There were people who believed the cover stories, and there were people who did not. For my part, I told my wife Joan where I was going (I thought), what I would be doing, and why — at least to the extent that I, myself, knew at the time. I knew that if I told her not to talk about it, she would not; and that she would use my cover story to explain my absence to friends and family — very probably improving vastly on my own version.

Some of the wives and families who believed the cover stories became confused, uncertain and unhappy as rumors began to circulate around Birmingham in the weeks following our departure. Some of the wives who did not believe the cover stories, and were unable to penetrate beyond the rumors, became even more apprehensive. It was a delicate situation and had to be handled by each individual in whatever way he thought would work best to maintain security. I knew that I could trust my wife. I also knew that if anything happened to me, there would have to be *another* cover story that could create problems for everyone concerned.

As it happened, four of our people lost their lives. A cover story was quickly fabricated to explain what had happened to them. The wives didn't believe the cover story. They *did* create problems, and were bitter and unhappy for a long time afterwards. Later, in Nicaragua, after the four men had been shot down, I was talking to Frank about how things might be going back at home. I told Frank that my wife had known all along approximately where I was and what I was doing, deliberately to obviate the kind of situation that was developing back in Birmingham. Frank acquiesced in my decision for full disclosure (more or less) at home — which is not to say that it would have worked for everyone.

Afer we had gone over our cover stories with Jake, he asked what cities we had chosen to be "from." I had chosen Washington where I had lived on two separate occasions when my father was on duty at the War Department. Washington, it seems, was prohibited. No one was allowed to be from Washington.

My second choice was New York. Put to a severe test, I would have had a hard time convincing anyone that I knew much about New York. Twenty years earlier I had shipped out of New York for China, working as a seaman on the United States Army transport *Republic*. During that period I learned how to take a subway from Brooklyn to Billy Minsky's Burlesque in Times Square, and an Orange Julius stand on 42nd Street. When I was in New York after returning from England in World War II, I lingered long enough to learn how to get from the Lexington Hotel to Leon and Eddie's nightclub on 52nd Street, and to navigate reasonably accurately back to the hotel.

Eventually we all received authentic documents establishing us, under our phony names, as residents of the cities of our choice.

When we finished with Jake, we went in to see Hoyt. Hoyt took care of the money, insurance, and the contractual details of our employment. Pilots were paid $2,200 per month and $600 per month additional for expenses. Other crew members were paid somewhat less. Insurance was available if we wanted it. The premiums would be deducted from our pay. The insurance provided a $15,000 death benefit and a monthly indemnity of $550 per month for life for the widow of anyone who lost his life. There was also a contract to be signed. I signed the contract and the insurance papers Hoyt put in front of me without reading them.

Hoyt asked how I wanted to be paid. There were several options. I could be paid in cash every month, or I could have the money deposited in my bank, or by any combination of the two. Also, I could draw all or any part of my first month's pay in advance. I decided that $500 would tide me over for a few days.

Hoyt opened an attaché case that seemed to be filled with nothing but one hundred dollar bills. He dealt five off the top of one of the stacks and passed them along to me with a receipt form. I also decided that my expense money would take care of me in the field, and I elected to have the $2,200 salary deposited in my bank every month. When I returned from Central America, I learned that this monthly deposit had been made by a transfer of funds from a bank in St. Louis. No check was involved, and the source of the funds was unknown to the bank in Birmingham. The St. Louis bank simply notified the Birmingham bank that it had funds for me and was transferring them to my account. Sneaky, but highly efficient.

When we had all finished with Jake and Hoyt, Al gave us our final instructions. We were to leave Birmingham during the final week and be checked into the hotel in Miami not later than Sunday night. Al instructed us to leave Birmingham singly, or in pairs. He wanted to avoid any impression of some kind of troop movement. We were expected to arrive at, and to check into the hotel the same way. Reservations had been made in the name of our New England electronics company. We shook hands all around and began to drift out of the building. Riley Shamburger and Hal McGee were in the parking lot outside.

"How'd you all make out, Buck?" Riley asked.

"We're all squared away. We've got to be in Miami by Sunday night. Are you two coming to Miami?"

"No. Hal and I have to go to Washington for a week. We'll see you when you get where you're going."

While we were talking, Bill Peterson and Al Walters appeared. Al looked like a cat that had just swallowed a couple of canaries.

"Do you know what this sonofabitch has got in his pocket?" Bill asked.

"No, what?"

"He's got 28 one hundred dollar bills."

When Al had learned that he could draw a full month's pay and expenses in advance, nothing less would do. He and Bill got in a car together and headed for the main gate, tires squealing.

"We'll be getting those two honchos out of jail in the morning," Riley said.

"Or out of some hospital," Hal said.

We had become an organized group, bound together by a common purpose, and restricted in our freedom to discuss our business with anyone but ourselves. None of us had known any of the others well, some not at all. Under the circumstances, it was natural that we would begin to congregate in the few days before our departure for Miami. Mostly, we met at a beer and barbecue joint close to the airport. We drank a lot of beer. We compared notes on cover stories. We fought old wars and told a lot of lies. We speculated endlessly on the invasion. Everyone had a new rumor every day, always right straight from the horse's mouth. Al Walters strove mightily to reduce his $2800 to a manageable level. We looked each other over and sized each other up.

Because we all wanted to delay departure from home until the last possible moment, almost all of us were on the same airplane from Birmingham to Atlanta, and from Atlanta to Miami. We pulled up to the McAlister Hotel in Miami in a string of taxis, one right behind the other. We were about as inconspicuous as a herd of elephants when we entered the lobby to check in — a fact that was noted and called to our attention in no uncertain terms later. In those days in Miami, a low profile was the uniform of the day.

If, from a distance of years, it seems unusual that rumors of a U.S.-sponsored invasion of Cuba should have been so easily generated and so readily accepted in early 1961, it should be noted that all through 1960 and the first weeks of 1961, the nation's news media were filled with stories of Cuban exiles' activities in Florida and Central America. Charges and counter charges were being hurled from all directions concerning the aggressive and hostile intentions of the United States government toward Fidel Castro and Cuba.

Most of the news media, and a large part of the general public had pictured Castro as a kind of modern political Robin Hood. The disenchantment was sudden and complete after he arrived in power in Havana. Immediately, he began to start each day by lining up a dozen or so political prisoners against the wall and shooting them. In the first few months after he came to power, Castro thus disposed of more than 450 former members of the Batista regime, and a large number of his own early supporters.

As early as April 1960, after only fifteen months in power, Castro had already inspired organized opposition among his fellow Cubans. The Movement of Revolutionary Recovery (MMR) got underway on April 10, 1960, with a call to Cubans to take up arms against the Castro government. Membership in the MMR included many of Castro's former supporters — in and out of his government. Throughout the hemisphere, governments were taking a closer look at Castro in order to determine what they had to deal with. While they were trying to decide, propaganda barrages were laid down by all sides.

On April 25, 1960, Cuban Foreign Minister Raul Roa announced that an armed invasion from Guatemala was imminent. He accused Guatemala's President Ydigoras of conspiring with the United Fruit Company.

On April 28, Guatemala severed diplomatic relations with Cuba. President Ydigoras said that Castro was preparing subversive moves against Guatemala, Honduras and Nicaragua.

March 17, 1960, has been reported as the date President Eisenhower made his decision to lend American support to an effort to overthrow the Castro regime in Cuba.

On May 1, following a May Day parade, Castro talked for three hours, telling 250,000 Cubans that the U.S. State Department had engineered a plot with Guatemala designed to accuse Cuba as a major aggressor before the OAS. He said the purpose of this plot was to justify the invasion of Cuba. He referred to President Ydigoras' "absurd charges" that troops were being trained in the Sierra Maestra to invade Guatemala. "We have the news," Castro said, "that the U.S. State Department is preparing an aggression against Cuba through Guatemala."

And so it went through the summer and fall of 1960. In May, President Ydigoras announced that he was initiating continuous guerrilla training maneuvers in answer to the threat of Cuban invasion. Ydigoras said that President Morales of Honduras had informed him that communist guerrilla bands were being organized and trained by Cubans on the Guatemala-Honduras border.

On July 7, 1960, Assistant Secretary of State A.A. Berle said: "For all practical purposes Cuba is just as much a communist nation as Hungary or North Korea. The island republic has been converted into not only a spearhead of Soviet and Chinese propaganda, but also a potential base for Soviet and Chinese power.

"The clique dominating Cuba intends direct aggression against the rest of Latin America with Soviet and Chinese support. The United States and any Latin American countries that care to join (I believe most would do so) should be prepared to oppose by all necessary means any movements or governments that are manipulated overtly or covertly by forces outside the hemisphere. What I am suggesting is not intervention but defense."

Three days later Premier Khrushchev got into the act. In a Moscow speech Khrushchev said that the USSR would retaliate with rockets if the United States intervened militarily in Cuba. "The United States even now is plotting insidious and criminal steps against Cuba," Khrushchev said.

To this President Eisenhower immediately responded that the United States would never permit "the establishment of a regime dominated by international communism in the western hemisphere." At the same time he accused Khrushchev of attempting to transform Cuba into a Soviet instrument, and he warned that definite action by the United States would be called for if Cuba, or any other country in the western hemisphere, fell under control of international communism.

There was nothing ambiguous in either of these statements. They said quite clearly what the attitude of the United States government was at that time, and what we intended to do about the situation rapidly developing in Cuba if it continued. It was at about this time that an American construction company, Thompson-Cornwall, began work on the 5,000-foot runway at an airfield at Retalhuleu, Guatemala.

The Retalhuleu air base was used to supply the Cuban exile force that was training in the mountains on the Pacific coast of Guatemala, and it was from this base that these troops, their equipment and supplies, were flown by the C-54 pilots in our group to the final staging base at Puerto Cabezas, Nicaragua. Obviously, the plans and decisions necessary to put this operation into effect had been made some months earlier.

Accusations, recriminations, charges and countercharges continued to fill the air. In Moscow on October 25, a commentator for the Soviet press agency, Tass, said that an invasion force equipped with American arms was building up in Guatemala. On the same day the Guatemalan government rejected an accusation by a student group in Quezaltenango (less than a hundred miles from Retalhuleu) that anti–Castro Cubans and North Americans were preparing an invasion of Cuba in Guatemalan territory.

On October 28, President Ydigoras said that "Guatemala does not need nor is it offering sites for foreign bases. Neither has any friendly nation requested permission to establish bases on national territory."

In the United Nations on November 1, Cuba proposed a debate on charges that the United States was backing an invasion plan. This proposal was voted down after a motion by the United States to send the proposal to the United Nations political committee for debate. Cuba and the Soviet block nations accused the United States of stalling maneuvers to give the United States time to complete plans for the invasion from bases in Florida and Guatemala.

By mid–November the existence and the activities at the air base in Retalhuleu had become widely known. In answer to questions about this base President Ydigoras said, ". . . it was one of several established in a program designed to reorient military training in Guatemala toward guerrilla warfare." He denied emphatically that the project was subsidized by the United States, and branded as "a lot of lies" reports that the base at Retalhuleu had been established with U.S. assistance as a training ground for military action in Cuba.

President Eisenhower severed diplomatic relations with Cuba on January 3, 1961. At the time, it was believed in some diplomatic circles that this move might lead the newly emerging nations of the world to believe that there was some basis for Cuban charges that the United States was planning an aggression against Cuba. State Department officials, however, did not share these views. It was their opinion that the Cuban foreign minister had nothing to back up his charges.

In the circumstances, deniability was no doubt necessary and to be expected. That the State Department would believe, if, in fact, it did, that the Cuban foreign minister "had nothing to back up his charges," is not credible. Foreign Minister Roa obviously knew what he was talking about. Everyone on Flagler Street in Miami, and everyone in the world with foreign service representatives in Guatemala knew what was in progress. A logical assumption is that the State Department had been deliberately insulated from policies and plans being made across the street in the White House.

Commenting on the break in U.S. diplomatic relations in January, Roa said:

> The purpose is obvious; to undermine and disfigure the character of the Cuban revolution in order to set the subjective and objective groundwork for direct military action; in other words, the glorious victory of Guatemala in 1954 is to be re-edited and repeated. At this moment Cuba is immediately threatened by invasion by the United States.
>
> Material from North America was airlifted to counterrevolutionary groups operating in the mountains ... camps of mercenaries are maintained in Florida and Central America and paid for with American dollars. The CIA foots the bill for a systematic campaign of calumny from different broadcasting stations, and this is part of the psychological warfare which has been unleashed in order to prepare conditions for a wide-scale assault.
>
> Although the Central Intelligence Agency has very often changed its plans and postponed them, we have accurate information that we are now facing the final blow.

To this statement U.S. Ambassador to the United Nations, James J. Wadsworth, replied on January 4,

> In these false and hysterical charges which have been laid before the Security Council by the Cuban government, we have a fresh reminder of the strategy of harassment by which they brought us — and I think definitely on purpose — to last night's decision.
>
> The United States has nothing to hide and nothing to fear from these charges. They are false and cannot stand the light of day. If anyone has reason to fear a debate on this subject it is the Cuban leaders themselves who have been crying "wolf" for the past six months over an alleged "imminent invasion" of their country, and thereby are fast making themselves ridiculous in the eyes of the rest of the world. I reject categorically the ridiculous charges of the Cuban government.

It was at about this time that I first talked to Riley Shamburger in Birmingham. Financial, logistical, and training support for the Cuban exiles was already firmly established. Air drops of munitions and supplies to guerrilla forces operating in the mountains inland from the Cuban port city of Trinidad were being made on a regular basis.

Controversy about Cuban exile activities had not been confined to the daily battle of words in the United Nations. The 1960 presidential election campaign had gotten underway in the summer and was building up steam during the fall months prior to election day in November. In a campaign speech on October 20, John F. Kennedy called for U.S. aid to freedom fighters inside Cuba and in exile "who are seeking to overthrow the Castro regime."

Two days later, On October 22, his opponent, Vice President Richard Nixon, said that Kennedy's statement was a "shockingly reckless proposal that might lead to World War III." In a speech at Chester, Pennsylvania, Nixon called Kennedy's proposal for United States government support for a revolution in Cuba the "most shockingly irresponsible proposal ever made in our history by a presidential candidate during a campaign."

On October 23, Nixon sent Kennedy a telegram, which he first released to the press, in which he said,

> . . . thus it is clear that you and I are diametrically opposed in a matter of great public interest, and one which the next president may have to deal with as soon as he assumes office. It is my firm belief that the course of action you propose is dangerously reckless. It violates U.S. government solemn commitments to the OAS and the UN not to interfere in the internal affairs of other members of these organizations. Your proposal will alienate every one of our sister American states . . . and give Khrushchev valid excuses to intervene on the side of the Castro government. If this happens your policy could lead to World War III.

This shot was fired by a candidate who fully expected to win the election and assume the office of president. Nixon was chairman of the National Security Council and, as such, was fully aware of the plans in progress by the administration to support an attempt to do exactly what candidate Kennedy proposed. He already knew that as president he would have to "deal with" the matter which he told Kennedy "could lead to World War III."

Americans are becoming more and more conditioned to put little faith in anything presidential candidates say during a political campaign. But for sheer policy hypocrisy it might be hard to find anything in the history of presidential politics to equal Nixon's attack on Kennedy's call for help in Cuba. In effect, Nixon believed that he could improve his chances to be elected by attacking a policy he was already committed to if *he* became president.

Kennedy's campaign strategists, spooked by the vehemence of Nixon's reaction, went on the air that night. Retreating immediately, Robert Kennedy said in a television speech that his brother's statement had been widely misinterpreted. "He is not suggesting armed intervention in Cuba," he said, "or the fact that we arm people so they can land in Cuba. Nothing in his statement indicates as much."

Activity at the airbase at Retalhuleu was increasing daily, as were reports of training camps in the mountains to the southeast. Although reporters were not permitted near these bases, B-26s and C-54s were very much in evidence at Retalhuleu. Formation flights of B-26s were almost a daily occurrence. Guatemalan authorities now admitted that U.S. personnel were being used as instructors, but they still insisted that those being trained were Guatemalan troops. The Guatemalan government said that there were Cubans present, but that they were also instructors.

The Guatemalan government also stressed the defensive nature of the training being carried on with financial and technical assistance of the United States, and it denied assertions by opponents of President Ydigoras that the military preparations in evidence were part of a plan for offensive action against Castro. In Washington on January 10, State Department press officer R. Lincoln White said in reply to a question about activities in Guatemala, "As to the report of a specific base, I know absolutely nothing."

During this same period, Miami residents who lived near the abandoned Opa-locka Navy Air Station north of the city were frequently awakened at night by the sound of low-flying aircraft taking off and landing at the blacked-out airfield.

When Miami newspapers began to carry reports of these activities, it became a practice with many Miami residents to drive out to the field at night to watch as unlighted four-engine aircraft landed and departed low over the tops of the cars parked on the perimeter road. Arriving aircraft came in out of the night with a sound of throttled engines overhead, brief outline of wings and fuselage against the blue flame of engine exhausts, and the squeal of rubber against concrete as the unlighted aircraft touched down on the darkened runway.

Questioned by a reporter about the night flights into and out of Opa-locka, Edward F. Ahrens, district director of the U.S. Border Patrol, said, "Nothing has come to my attention."

Cuban exiles who had been pouring into Miami by the thousands for more than a year had created a "little Havana" at the Flagler Street and Biscayne Boulevard intersection in downtown Miami. Recruiting activities in this area were poorly disguised. The forthcoming effort to overthrow Castro was the subject of constant speculation and conversation. Among the thousands of Cubans who had found their way out of Cuba to Florida were hundreds of agents and informers for the Castro government. Telephone communication between Miami and Havana at that time was simple, and as close as the pay phone on any corner. Whatever anyone knew and talked about in Miami, Castro also knew.

This, then, was the sequence of events, some of the dialogue, and much of the activity that preceded the arrival of the group of airmen from Alabama at the McAlister Hotel in Miami.

Two years after the brief engagement at the Bay of Pigs, Robert Kennedy said that the critical decisions made by the president at the time of the invasion were motivated by the "surfacing of the role of the United States during the first hours of the invasion." Even the most casual examination of newspaper stories and other published reports which had accumulated for more than a year before the invasion, made it abundantly clear that the role of the United States government had "surfaced" long before April 15, 1961.

Florida

When we all crowded up to the desk at the McAlister Hotel, looking self-conscious and conspiratorial, the clerk craned his head as if to see who might be behind us in the lobby. No doubt he thought we were trying to sneak women up to our rooms. When we asked for our reservations in the name of the company we were supposed to be representing, the desk clerk's suspicion was replaced by an attitude of long-suffering resignation. I think he knew that we were probably going to be with him for awhile, and would be cluttering up his lobby all day long. He was right.

All of our rooms were on the same floor and were connecting. Everyone parked his luggage and within 30 minutes we were all crowded together in one room. Our instructions had been to check in and wait. We sat up "waiting" until three in the morning. We were very green at the time.

Next morning we sat around the lobby, wandered in and out of the hotel coffee shop and bar, and strolled around on Biscayne Boulevard where there were more people speaking Spanish than English. Downtown Miami was filled with Cuban exiles. They gathered on street corners and stood around outside small cafes and bars talking excitedly, gesturing wildly, and contributing greatly to the atmosphere of tension and intrigue that pervaded Miami in 1961.

Shortly after noon, Red Cornish, Sandy Sanders, and Leo Baker disappeared in search of friends of Red who lived on Miami Beach and who, according to Red, "used to own a big yacht." Three or four men went up the street to a movie. Another group staked out a dark corner in the cocktail lounge. Neilson, Chapman, Ealey, King and I settled down on a veranda just off the lobby where we could keep an eye on the pedestrian traffic on Biscayne Boulevard. Gordon wanted to know if we were going to sit around all afternoon ogling young girls. We assured him that we were.

Gordon Neilson had been a fighter pilot and an instructor at the Air Force's instrument school at Valdosta, Georgia. Although he stood less than six feet tall, he gave the impression of being tall, lean and lanky. He was what is often described as "rope thin." He looked like a long-distance runner, which is exactly what he was, not in a competitive, professional sense, but in a personally, absolutely dedicated to running commitment that let nothing get in his way.

Gordon ran only in the interest of what he called "staying in shape." He didn't drink. He didn't smoke, and if he could, he ran at least five miles every day. There were few times and circumstances where he let anything interfere with his daily canter. Even in Retalhuleu, and in Puerto Cabezas, Gordon went out every afternoon and chugged up and down the runway. Because the temperature and humidity were always in the high 90s, this was a painful performance, even to watch.

Gordon guarded his money almost as carefully as he guarded his health. He was pleasant in his parsimony. He took a lot of ribbing with unruffled good humor. But he *was* insistent. If there was a restaurant tab or a grocery bill to be shared, it was shared absolutely equally, even if it meant getting a nickel changed into five pennies in order to carry out the accounting to the last decimal place. And anyone who added a tip to a tab shared by Gordon did so at his own risk and expense. The most important thing about Gordon, though, was that he was as meticulous about his flying as he was about his health and his money. He was the most skillful and dependable pilot in our group, and when the time came to fly, Gordon was always ready to go, no matter what the circumstances.

Fred Ealey was a loner. No one ever got to know him. He insisted on a room by himself in Miami, and he lived alone when we moved to Ft. Lauderdale later. Fred was big. He looked as if he belonged in somebody's front four. His short, straight black hair grew so low on his forehead it almost met the bushy black eyebrows that came together at the bridge of his nose. The bone structure of Fred's face was massive and so arranged that Gordon and I nicknamed him Pithecanthropus Erectus. If all this suggests that Fred was sullen, he was not. But where the rest of us were garrulous about our previous histories and past experiences, Fred had nothing to say, other than his home was somewhere in Louisiana (it may or may not have been). No one ever learned anything about his background as a pilot or through what channels or connections he had become a part of our contingent. There may have been some freakish foul-up, for it eventually became apparent that Fred had not only never flown a C-54, the chances are that he had never flown *anything* with four engines.

Phil Chapman and Ernie King had known each other during the Korean War when they had been attached to the same transport squadron. It was through Ernie that General Doster had recruited Phil. Like the rest of us, he had no current military connections. Unlike the rest of us, he had not flown since the end of the Korean War, a period of nearly ten years. Ten years is a long time to lay off flying. Phil stayed "behind the power curve" throughout most of the operation.

Phil was the successful manager of an insurance agency in a large midwestern city. Like Fred, he may have bitten off more than he could chew. I think he was intrigued mostly with the *idea* of what we were doing. He liked being a part of the act, and he felt that he was well cast in his role — however it was that he saw it. But I believe that Phil looked forward to the curtain call with far more anticipation than to the show itself.

Phil was tall, dark, handsome, and very finicky. He was the kind who never found the service in a restaurant quite up to his standards. He made a big deal of ordering Chablis with his pompano. (I don't think he knew the name of any other white wine.) The filet mignon was never rare enough, and no bartender ever made a martini dry enough to suit him. Phil was an ex-tiger. He enjoyed fond memories of a day long past when he prowled the jungle with the best of them. Now, he was a middle-aged tomcat who still sounded good on the back fence, but was a little short on performance when all the cats squared off in the alley.

Ernie was glad to have Phil along. Ernie had a compulsion to establish himself. He wanted to create some kind of pecking order in our group with himself at the head of it. He was already established with Phil from the days they had served together in the Korean War. Now it was necessary for him to apply his personal criteria for seniority to everyone else and to locate everyone on a chain that led downward from him.

Ernie's sole criteria for leadership was "flying time." He wanted to believe that if he had more "flying time" than anyone else, this would automatically project him into the position of leadership he so obviously craved. If some little green men had suddenly appeared with a request to "take me to your leader," Ernie would have wanted them marched straight to him. Ernie lobbied persistently. He diverted every conversation, on any subject, into channels where he could discover how many hours in the air each of us had logged. Whoever the high man turned out to be, Ernie was going to have at least a thousand hours more.

There was no requirement, of course, in our setup for anyone to assume "authority," nor any opportunity to exercise it. We had been hired for one purpose, to drive airplanes. We all recognized Ernie's compulsion, however, and we went out of our way to nurture it. Instead of waiting around the hotel for hours on end for someone to "contact" us, we let Ernie do it. When we went over to Miami Beach for a swim, we left Ernie in charge at the hotel to make the contact and to pass on all the instructions to us. Wherever we went we found a telephone and called back to give Ernie a number where we could be reached. He loved it. So did we. And, of course, we made certain that *no one* had more flying time than Ernie.

Ernie's first opportunity to round everyone up came on our fourth afternoon in Miami. I was on the beach with some of the other pilots when his call came. *Ernie had been contacted.* We were all to meet with a company representative at eight o'clock that night at the hotel.

The company representative's name was Jim. (There were a lot of people in the CIA named Jim.) Beginning the next morning we would all be required to undergo the "black box" treatment, as Jim referred to the polygraph test. Jim said that if there were any of us who didn't want to take the test, for any reason, we were free to decline and drop out of the program with no questions asked and no hard feelings. I believe that this suggestion was itself a part of the treatment. Springing a lie detector test on us, out of the blue, may have been designed to eliminate even the necessity for the test if there were any among us who had reason to believe that this was an obstacle he would rather not face. No one rose to the bait but, as it turned out later, there was one of our group who may have had second thoughts but decided to give it a try anyway.

Jim couldn't tell us anything about when we might be moving on. His advice was to sit tight. We'd be hearing something in a few days. Several of us were running out of money, so we suggested to Jim that if our stay in Miami were going to be extended for more than a few days, it might be well for him to pump up our money clips. Jim left the room and came back with the inevitable attaché case filled with one hundred dollar bills. Those of us who had been too modest in anticipating our needs before leaving Birmingham drew another advance.

If the handling of money sounds haphazard and random, it actually was not. All of the advances of money at intervals, by various individuals, was accounted for to the penny in our final settlements. At the time, we were all naturally entranced by what seemed to be an inexhaustible supply of one hundred dollar bills on which we could draw at will. But somewhere beyond our ken there was an accounting office that managed to keep track of the cash flow.

The polygraph testing took two days. Ernie and Jim set up a schedule that allowed one hour for each man. As with so many of our company contacts, when the tests were finished, we never saw "Jim" again.

My turn on the machine came on the afternoon of the first day. As each man finished his test, he notified the next man on the list. We went up to a room on the eighth floor of the hotel. We were admitted by a professorial looking gentleman who explained that he was a member of a Chicago firm retained to conduct the tests by our employer in accordance with their requirements.

These introductory remarks were made to establish his ignorance of the nature of our employer's business and, obviously, to cut off any possible discussion of matters other than the business immediately at hand. By now, of course, we were all thoroughly adjusted to operating in these vacuums where no one ever knew anything about anything.

The professor explained briefly how the machine worked and how effective it was. To demonstrate, after I was all hooked up, he asked me my wife's name — which is Joan. "Now," he said, "I'm going to use a series of names including your wife's name. I will ask you each time if your wife is named so-and-so. I want you to answer 'no' to each question. I will show you how this thing works."

We began the demonstration.

"Is your wife's name Pat?"

"No."

"Is your wife's name Gloria?"

"No."

"Is your wife's name Joan?"

"No."

And so on, through a series of names. When we were finished, he showed me where a needle writing in red ink on a drum of graph paper had gone crazy when I answered "no" to the question "Is your wife's name Joan?"

Needless to say, I was suitably impressed. Here was a machine that could detect even a make-believe lie designed to deceive no one and uttered without any emotional stress that I was aware of.

Next, the professor explained that we would run through a series of questions without having the polygraph switched on. In this first interrogation I was free to answer each question at length, qualifying and explaining anything I wished. After which, with the polygraph operating, the same questions would be asked again, this time prefaced by "other than what you have already told me." Answers to the final questions would be a simple "yes" or "no" — "no" being the only correct answer.

Sample questions were: "Have you ever lived or traveled in a foreign country?" "Have you ever been a member of the communist party or any organization affiliated with the communist movement?" "Have you ever been arrested or convicted of a felony?" "Have you ever practiced homosexuality or bestiality?" "Have you ever used an assumed name, an alias?" "Do any of your relatives live in a foreign country?" Etc., etc.

The professor explained that my employers were not interested in passing judgment, and that my continuing employment was not necessarily related to my answers, but if there *were* anything in my background that could be used against me by anyone hostile or unfriendly to me, my employers wanted that information in order to eliminate the possibility of its being a potential source of pressure against me. In other words, if I were, say, a homosexual, or if I had a prison term somewhere in my background, the company wanted to know about it, not as a reason to fire me, but to eliminate a potential for blackmail and other forms of extortion.

It sounded reasonable enough, but I doubt if it was really all that cut and dried. There was no reason why the company would risk *any* degree of exposure with people at our level. As a matter of fact, one of our group departed a short time after the polygraph test. It may be that the "black box" had uncovered something that the company decided it did not want to buy.

One significant difference between the final test and the rehearsal was a long, 15- or 20-second pause between each question. After you had answered "no" to a question, that long pause would make it hard for someone who had lied to divert his attention effectively enough to deceive the polygraph. That's the way it worked for me, although I was not trying to deliberately hide anything. During one of those long pauses, I remembered something I had failed to respond to in the rehearsal.

The question was, "Other than what you have already told me, have you ever used an assumed name, an alias?"

My response was again "no," but in the pause that followed, I suddenly recalled an evening 25 years earlier when my brother and I had picked up a couple of girls down around the Washington Monument. For some perverse reason, which escapes me, we spent the evening with them as the "Abernathy" brothers. The polygraph needle started to climb the wall and we had to halt proceedings while I explained the incident.

"See what I mean?" said the professor.

We finished with the polygraph tests the next afternoon. That night we were called together again by our leader, Ernie, to meet with "Jack." By now Ernie was well established as our "bell cow." Sweating and twinkling like a chubby little gnome, Ernie bustled around the hotel all day long, happy as a brand new lance corporal.

Jack had two sets of orders, one for the B-26 pilots, another for the C-54 crews. The two groups were separating the next day. Bill Peterson, Al Walters, Don Gordon, Joe Hinkle, Pete Ray and Ron Smith were leaving Miami the next night for a flight to Guatemala. They were instructed to set out first thing in the morning and buy new clothes. They were given a list of items they would need: two or three pairs of khaki trousers, three or four pairs of shorts, T-shirts, underwear, a light jacket, socks, high-lace boots, and a good hunting knife. Jack emphasized that the boots and knife should be of the best quality. When they had made these purchases the men were to return to the hotel, cut all the labels off the clothing, don one set, pack the rest into a plain duffle bag, and be ready to leave the hotel that night at eight o'clock. Everything else, other than shaving gear, was to be packed into the suitcases we had arrived with in Miami.

The C-54 crews were told to rent an automobile next morning and drive to Ft. Lauderdale. There we were to find living quarters that could be rented for a couple or three weeks. After which we were to report back to the hotel in Miami.

There were too many of us for one car, so we rented two. Ernie King, Phil Chapman, Gordon Neilson, Earl Carter and I used one car. Leo Baker, Jack Vernon, Sandy Sanders, Wade Gray and Red Cornish used the other. Our loner, Fred Ealey, rented a car for himself and found his own living quarters in Ft. Lauderdale.

We made our plans for the day next morning in the hotel coffee shop. We decided that if suitable accommodations could be found in Ft. Lauderdale, the pilots would take an apartment together, and the other crew members would take another. This arrangement was logical enough, but Leo immediately sensed some kind of class distinction shaping up.

"The next thing you know, you bastards will be trying to pull rank on us."

"Why don't you get your ass off your shoulder, Leo?" Gordon asked. "If it will prove anything, I'll be glad — let me make that *willing* — to bunk with you."

"Go to hell, Gordon, you're not my type."

Another argument developed over whether we should find accommodations on the beach or somewhere in town. Opinions ranged all the way from Gordon's, who thought the YMCA at $1.50 a day would serve our purposes, to Phil's who liked the idea of a suite at a beachfront hotel. Since we were paying our own expenses, we compromised. We agreed to meet in Ft. Lauderdale, cool off for an hour or two, and then explore an area where there were numerous modestly appointed apartment-hotels located two or three blocks from the beach.

After the drive from Miami to Ft. Lauderdale it took us a little longer to cool off than we had anticipated. It was well up into the afternoon before we set out in search of living quarters. As luck would have it, there was a vacancy in the first place we stopped, a small, two-story apartment building with ten one-bedroom units, a tiny "swimming pool" in the back yard, and one vacancy.

The owners were a Mr. and Mrs. Harding. The Hardings had retired and moved from Indiana to Florida a couple of years earlier. For the most part, their tenants were also retirees who came down to Florida for two weeks or a month every winter.

We explained to the Hardings that we were engaged in aviation electronics research and would be flight testing our products at the Ft. Lauderdale airport for a few weeks. They readily agreed to put five of us in their vacant apartment. A call to an apartment owner across the street soon had the other five men established in a similar unit. Each apartment had one bedroom with two single beds, a living room with two sofas that made up into beds, a bathroom, kitchenette and dining area. Each group solved the problem of the fifth man by adding a folding cot which could be unlimbered at night in the living room. This kind of high-density occupancy was not unusual in the winter season when rates were at their highest. We paid a week's rent in advance, said that we would move in the next day or two, and were on our way back to Miami by five o'clock that afternoon.

When we arrived at the hotel, we found the B-26 group packed, dressed in fatigues and boots, and getting ready to check out. "Eric" was now in charge.

"Gentlemen, you're late," Eric said. "These men are scheduled to depart the airport in an hour. Have you found suitable accommodations in Ft. Lauderdale?"

Eric was precise and formal. We learned later that he was an Air Force Major on detached duty with the company. He was devoid of humor, and he took himself very, very seriously. In spite of the fact that most of us were several years older than Eric, and more experienced pilots, he always spoke to us as if he were addressing a detachment of aviation cadets. We had the feeling that he would have liked for us to pop to attention when he entered the room. Perversely, we went to the opposite extremes. Whenever he showed up at our apartment in Ft. Lauderdale, we made a big production of popping open cans of beer, mixing drinks with a loud rattling of ice and glasses, stifling yawns, and stretching out flat on the sofas and floor while he pontificated. In general, we did everything possible to convey an attitude of not-quite-polite and somewhat bored attention.

For his part, Eric made it obvious that he did not *really* think of us as "gentlemen," and that in addressing us as such he was only bestowing a kind of courtesy title on the group that in no way reflected our individual social standings.

"I've seen a lot of GI bastards in my time," said Red Cornish, "but this guy is the goddamndest tin soldier I've *ever* run into."

"I'll bet the sonofabitch sleeps at attention," Leo said.

We gave Eric the addresses of our apartments in Ft. Lauderdale.

"You will check out of here in the morning," Eric said, "and proceed to Ft. Lauderdale. Wait there for my further instructions. I will be back in contact with you in the next day or two. Now gentlemen," turning to the B-26 group, "I think we had better be on our way."

We shook hands all around and Eric and the six B-26 pilots filed out of the hotel room, suitcases in one hand, duffle bags slung over their shoulders, shiny new boots creaking down the hallway.

"That is certainly an inconspicuous group," I said.

"About as inconspicuous as a herd of rhinos," Fred Ealey said.

The B-26 pilots flew directly from the Opa-locka air base to Retalhuleu. It was several weeks before the rest of us joined them in Guatemala.

Next morning we checked out of the hotel and "proceeded" to Ft. Lauderdale to await Eric's further instructions. We occupied ourselves with trips to the supermarket, liquor stores, and the beach.

Mrs. Harding rustled up a barbecue grill from her storage room. Gordon had a secret recipe for barbecue sauce and he therefore put himself in charge of all barbecuing. The sauce wasn't bad, but instead of buying sirloin or T-bone steaks, Gordon bought thin chuck roasts and tried to pass them off as "steaks."

Gordon put on a sweat suit and ran up and down the beach for an hour every afternoon while the rest of us sprawled out on the sand. We referred to this period as "ogle time." Fred Ealey checked in with us at the apartment a couple of times a day. Otherwise, he didn't fraternize. We never solved the mystery of Fred and what seemed to us to be his company-sanctioned independence. There was speculation that he may have been a "spy" for the company. The other speculation was that he had been living with a girlfriend. Gordon saw this as so unlikely as to be unworthy of any serious consideration. "Anything that would get into bed with him has already been extinct for twenty-five thousand years," he said.

Late in the afternoon of the third day Eric came to the apartment with "Ray." Only Gordon and Ernie were in the apartment when they arrived. Fred had checked in earlier and departed. Phil was a few blocks away at a Turkish nightclub he had discovered. He had fallen in "love" with one of the belly dancers in the floor show, and was trying to get some busboys to open the place at four o'clock in the afternoon. Maybe he thought the belly dancer would show up for rehearsal. Earl Carter and I were at the beach. When we came in Eric, Ray, Ernie and Gordon were sitting around the dinette table. Eric introduced us to Ray, but it turned out that Earl and Ray already knew one another. They had been in the same class at flying school as cadets and had served together for a short time on active duty. This was an unanticipated development, and it may have been responsible for Earl's sudden departure. When we came in from flying a few days later, Earl, who had not gone with us, was packing his bags. All he knew, and all he ever learned, was that Eric had come by in the morning and told him that he had orders from Washington that Earl was to return home.

Earl said that Eric couldn't give him any reason for his sudden elimination from the operation. The only thing Eric ever told us was that he "had been instructed to send Carter home." We thought it may have had something to do with the polygraph test back in Miami, but it may also have been because Earl had "uncovered" Ray. Earl didn't seem to be too unhappy.

Eric explained that Ray would act as our instructor for a short period of orientation flying on the C-54 beginning first thing in the morning. However, it was not Ray who picked us up the next morning at the apartment, but "Mac" and "Les." Ray had been reassigned, which probably had something to do with running into Earl Carter. We didn't see him again until April in Retalhuleu where he arrived to assist in the airlift of the Cuban invasion forces from Retalhuleu to Puerto Cabezas.

Mac was a pilot in the Air Force on duty with the company. Les was a petty officer and flight engineer in the Navy, also detached to the company. Les would be responsible for instruction of our flight engineers and two radio operators.

We set up a schedule of six-hour training periods that started at six o'clock every morning, or every evening, depending on the availability of the aircraft. Three pilots and two flight engineers were on each flight along with our instructor, Mac. Each pilot flew for a two-hour period.

Jack Vernon and Wade Gray, who were radio operators, went along often enough to become familiar with the radar and radio systems. Neither they nor any of the rest of us, including Mac, could figure out what their eventual roles and responsibilities would be.

In 1961 communications between aircraft in flight and between aircraft and ground stations no longer required the services of radio operators tapping out and receiving messages in Morse code. It was, and is, a matter of picking up a microphone and talking into it the way you would a telephone. At the pilot's end, conversations are monitored through an on-board receiver hooked up to a speaker and/or headsets in the cockpit. Radio navigation involves little more than tuning in a frequency, setting a desired heading on an instrument panel dial, and keeping a needle centered until you arrive over the station you're tuned to. The pilot can handle all of this alone. It does not require assistance from a radio operator. As for maintenance and repair of radio equipment, very little can be accomplished in flight.

Late one afternoon we returned from flying to find "Ferd" Dutton unpacking his bags. Ferd was not his name. I started calling him Ferd as short for Ferdinand Magellan after he gave me a 40-degree heading correction one night three hours into a flight from Puerto Cabezas to Florida. (Prior to this massive course correction, Ferd's navigation had us headed straight for Cuba.)

Ferd identified himself as a navigator. He said he was from California. We didn't know what he was supposed to do any more than we knew why we had a couple of radio operators. By now, however, we had completely accommodated to company practices. We never asked anyone any questions about himself. But whatever else Ferd may have been, he was no navigator.

Ferd did have one distinction. He was the only member of our small company to set foot on Cuban soil — and get back out, that is. Ferd was on the C-46 that landed at Girón on Wednesday morning, April 19. I'll guarantee it was not Ferd's navigation that got them up to the Bay of Pigs. They barely had time to get out before the field was taken by Castro's people.

The C-54 is the military version of the Douglas DC-4, a four-engine transport that first saw service in World War II. The Air Transport Command used the C-54 in every theater of operations. After the Japanese occupied Burma and cut off the Burma Road, C-54s played a major role in a massive airlift across the Hump to supply Chiang Kai-shek's armies and General Chennault's 14th Air Force with the equipment and supplies they needed to stay in action against the Japanese, and to prevent the otherwise inevitable conquest of India. President Roosevelt's famous "Sacred Cow" was a C-54.

A fully loaded C-54 weighs 36.5 tons. The span from wing tip to wing tip measures 40 yards, almost half the length of a football field, and from nose to tail it measures 94 feet. Four engines turning three-blade props generate a total of 5,800 horsepower. Sometimes, almost a mile of paved runway is required to reach a speed where the aircraft will lift off the ground and fly.

The cockpit of a large aircraft is an engine control room. It is also an electrical, radio and communications center, and it is the captain's and the navigator's bridge. There are controls that meter the flow of fuel to the engines; controls to maintain constant cylinder-head and oil temperatures; controls to maintain proper fuel-air ratios; controls to vary the pitch of the propeller blades; controls to regulate carburetor air temperature; controls to provide extra engine boost at high altitudes where the air is thin. For every set of controls there are corresponding instruments which display any deviation from normal operating limits and warn the pilots of possible malfunctions.

In addition to engine instruments and controls, there are flight instruments by which pilots can determine precisely the attitude and movement of the aircraft in relation to the earth below. Often, at night or in bad weather, there is no visual reference to the earth or to the sky. There is no physical sensation of speed or motion. There is nothing but the instruments on the panel to convince the pilot that he is, indeed, three miles above the surface of the earth, that the wings of the aircraft are level with an invisible horizon, and that the aircraft is moving through the air at a constant rate of speed directly toward a specific geographical point somewhere miles ahead.

Forty-nine instruments cover almost every inch of the five-foot wide instrument panel in a C-54. There are also 74 switches on the electric and generator control panel. A forest of levers and mechanical controls projects from the pedestal between the two pilots' seats. Behind them, the navigator's station is a small table surrounded by banks of radio transmitters and receivers, frequency control panels, heading and position indicators, a large radar screen, and a five-foot high panel of switches and circuit breakers.

It is possible by means of such highly sophisticated radio navigation systems to depart the end of one runway and arrive at the end of another, a thousand or more miles distant, without ever seeing the earth below, and without catching a glimpse of the sun or stars above. And if you don't want to hand-fly the aircraft, an automatic pilot will fly it and do the navigating for you.

Our purpose in Ft. Lauderdale was not to learn how to fly four-engine aircraft (except, maybe, for Pithecanthropus Erectus). Our daily flights were for recurrent training designed to bring us back, hopefully, to a high degree of proficiency on a particular aircraft, the C-54, and to redevelop pilot skills required to fly the aircraft with no leeway for errors of judgment or technique under conditions that would demand maximum performance from both aircraft and crew.

All of this was accomplished at a loss of about ten pounds per man per flight. We practiced emergency procedures over and over again. In-flight fires, as well as electrical system, radio and engine failures were simulated on every training flight. Holding 35 tons of airplane straight and level with two engines out on the same side requires as much physical strength as it does skill. We spent hours flying at night, practicing approaches and landings at a small, abandoned World War II training field in the Everglades west of Miami. "Everglades International" was not only abandoned, it was also without runway lights. One flare pot was placed at each end of the runway.

Landing lights on the aircraft could not be used. The runway was short. Consequently, approach speeds had to be controlled precisely, so as to touch down on the approach end of the runway, not somewhere halfway down its length, leaving insufficient runway ahead to brake to a stop before running off into the swamp.

It was hairy, but all of this precision flying was related to what we would be required to do routinely when we arrived in Central America.

Sooner or later, the regular pattern of these night flights into and out of the abandoned airstrip was bound to attract attention. One night we had come to a complete stop on the runway and were in the process of turning the aircraft around for a takeoff in the opposite direction. Two headlights appeared at the far end of the field moving toward us down the runway. Mac flipped on the landing lights, and I opened the throttles wide. I had a brief glimpse of a green patrol car with a large badge painted on the front door panel careening off the runway as we passed a few feet overhead. We returned to Ft. Lauderdale and flew no more that night. Two nights later we were back at the practice field. We continued to use it without interruption from local authorities.

It is interesting to speculate on how, and through what channels, word was passed to the sheriff of the county where our practice strip was located. Whatever these channels of communication were, they were effective, although I feel sure that the local sheriff's curiosity was never completely satisfied.

At Ft. Lauderdale we kept the aircraft on a ramp at the far side of the field from the airport terminal where commercial operations were conducted. By now we had all been issued business cards identifying us as representatives of the New England electronics company. Normally our activities, all of the flying in and out, day and night, would have attracted the attention of Immigration, Customs, the Border Patrol, the FAA, the FBI, and all local law enforcement agencies. No one ever came near us.

For the final ten days before we left Ft. Lauderdale, we practiced not only emergency procedures and blacked-out approaches and landings at "Everglades International," we also flew all over the state of Florida at an altitude of 200 feet at night, and without running lights. Even in broad daylight, flying at more than 200 miles per hour, 200 feet is awfully close to the ground. On a dark night at 200 feet you feel as if you are a part of the highway traffic. Although 200 feet will clear all natural terrain obstacles, it won't clear them by much. And the state of Florida is studded with radio antennas that rise much higher than 200 feet. The concentration required to maintain an exact altitude to avoid flying into the ground, plus the eye strain associated with watching for the blinking red lights that marked the location of soaring antennas, left us wringing wet.

In addition to the many hours we spent flying, we also spent many hours gathered around the dinette table in our apartment studying the C-54 flight manual. The flight manual contained everything there was to know about the C-54 — detailed descriptions of flight characteristics, performance charts and schematics of fuel, oil, hydraulic and electrical systems. A good working knowledge of an aircraft's systems and capabilities contributes immeasurably to the confidence and peace of mind of the crew, particularly when you are far out at sea with landfall many miles ahead.

Red Cornish was much better informed than the rest of us. He was an experienced flight engineer on C-54s. He had a thorough knowledge, both theoretical and practical, of the aircraft's systems. He could study and quickly interpret all the multi-colored schematics in the manual. He could preconceive all manner of possible malfunctions and emergency situations, describe their visual manifestations on the instrument panels in the cockpit, and prescribe the proper crew corrective responses. A good crew chief has saved the skins of many pilots.

Red had other talents not associated with the operation and maintenance of a C-54. During our brief stay at the hotel in Miami, Red had found his friend with the 60-foot yacht and handsome home on Miami Beach. Red quickly organized a second career for himself as first mate on the yacht, and he became a member in good standing in Miami Beach social circles which were devoted to boating, booze and (according to him) broads.

When we had to fly at night, Red was usually gone from the apartment by eight the next morning. When we returned from flying in the middle of the afternoon, most of us dissolved into pools of sweat and lay around the apartment for a couple of hours before reviving sufficiently to make it out to the small pool in back of the apartment, or wander down to the beach. Not Red. Red hit the shower and was on his way to Miami within 30 minutes. He would emerge from the apartment across the street absolutely immaculate in gray trousers, blue shirt, white tie and two-tone shoes. A light blue blazer hung in the back seat of the car. Freshly shaven, without a hair out of place, Red positively glistened in the bright Florida sunshine as he struck out for the Miami Beach marina — followed, I must say, by a lot of envious eyes.

Red never missed a flight, however, and, unlike Phil, he never showed the slightest wear and tear from his extracurricular activities.

We all surmised that Phil must have gotten married right out of high school to a wife who had kept him on a very short leash ever since. Given a newfound freedom from domestic restraints, Phil tended to go a little mad. The Turkish nightclub Phil discovered on our first night in Ft. Lauderdale, and more specifically the doe-eyed and pneumatic young belly dancer from Brooklyn who worked in the floor show, kept Phil in a perpetual state of excitement — and exhaustion. Unhappily for Phil, this quickly flowering friendship could only be cultivated between two o'clock in the morning when the belly dancer got off work, and six o'clock in the morning when Phil had to report to the flight line. There were mornings when he wasn't scheduled to fly, and on those days the "cultivating" usually continued right through to the following evening when the nightclub opened its doors at six o'clock. On those days, or nights, when Phil had to fly, he came straight from his Garden of Allah to the airport where we hoisted him into the aircraft and onto one of the bunks aft of the cockpit. We always scheduled him for the last of the three two-hour periods so that he could nap for four hours before having to address himself to the exigencies of the cockpit. We did this more out of consideration for our own hides than from sympathy for Phil's obviously terminal condition.

As far as I know, the only time Phil got any sleep while we were in Ft. Lauderdale was in the aircraft — except for one three-day period when the belly dancer was confined to the hospital with an abdominal disorder. (The demands of her art precluded an operation.) Leo wanted to make book on the chances for Phil's survival. He suggested that we form a pool to see who could come closest to predicting the day and hour on which Phil would expire. Phil made it, but I don't believe by a wide margin.

Eric showed up at the apartment periodically. Once we passed word through Mac that some of us were running out of money again. Eric came by with the usual attaché case stuffed with one hundred dollar bills. On another occasion he came by to make sure we had acquired, and to inspect, the de-labeled clothing and equipment required at our final destination.

None of us ever saw Eric, or Mac and Les, "socially." We didn't even know where they lived. We had a telephone number where we could reach Eric if the need arose. There was no need for socializing, of course, and if they wanted to keep everything on a strictly businesslike and professional basis, that was their prerogative, and it was also fine with us. It may even have been a company policy. However, there was a lack of ordinary friendliness in our relationship with Eric that seemed to go beyond the bounds of any company policy, and even beyond the restrictions of his own limited personality. I may have discovered what this was all about when I ran into Eric in a bar one night. He was alone. There were very few people in the bar, and it would have been senseless not to sit down next to him. Eric was pretty well up into the sauce, which surprised me, and he talked too much, which also surprised me. In the course of an ensuing conversation, Eric conceded that we—meaning our Birmingham group—"wash genumum" and not a bunch of "professional thugsh" like some people he had to deal with. The bar was beginning to fill. Eric had a considerable start on me, and it seemed wise not to hang around. The thought occurred to me later that maybe Eric and Mac didn't know any more about us than we did about them; that perhaps the policy of the company was a two-way street and no matter what the level of authority might be, right up to Allen Dulles, no one knew anything he didn't absolutely need to know. Conceivably, Eric and Mac knew nothing about our backgrounds or the details of our employment. Whatever the answer, it seemed likely that Eric had had business in the past with people whom he did not admire or respect, and with whom he had no desire to associate in any way other than what was required by the job at hand. Perhaps Eric had assumed from the beginning that we belonged to some such category of hired help already familiar to him. In any case, while this encounter provided an interesting sidelight, whatever it was that he thought was unimportant because we were about to bid Eric a permanent farewell.

Late one afternoon Eric arrived at the apartment while we were participating in Gordon's steak ritual. Any one of us was permitted to broil a steak in the oven. When we moved outdoors to the charcoal grill by the pool, however, Gordon became high priest. He was the only person entrusted with the rites he performed. Only he knew the secret formula for the sauce and its application to the burnt offering he tended. The broiler was Gordon's altar. No one was permitted to approach until commanded to do so. When the command came, needless to say, we felt that we should have gone forward on our hands and knees to accept our portions.

Eric brought the news that we were to leave next day for "down south." He instructed us to pack our gear and leave Ft. Lauderdale the next morning in time to be in Miami and checked into the Gateway Motel not later than five o'clock in the afternoon.

Eric stayed to share one of Gordon's steaks. He seemed suitably impressed. He said that it was a pity Gordon was not as well qualified on the C-54 as he was on the charcoal grill. This was a lugubrious attempt at light banter, but it was as close as Eric could come to unbending from his usual rigid formality.

We left Ft. Lauderdale the next day at noon. Mr. and Mrs. Harding seemed genuinely sorry to see us go. I think that they had hoped we might stay until after the annual Easter assault on the city by vacationing college students. We got out just under the wire. The Hardings were a nice old couple. Unlike many nice old couples who retire to the management of small apartment-hotels in Florida, they were not overburdened with curiosity about their guests. Not once in all the time we were their guests did they ask difficult questions or express undue interest in the activities of the five men who occupied apartment 21A, who flew airplanes everyday with the five men who lived across the street, and who came and went at all hours of the day and night.

When we first checked in with the Hardings we said that we were flight-checking new radio and electronic equipment manufactured by our New England employer. We were not overly enthusiastic about this story, but perhaps it was more credible than we thought. At that time no one could fly an airplane of any kind into or out of Florida without first filing a flight plan. Border Patrol and Customs people were stationed at almost every airport in Florida to prevent flights or any related activity in behalf of, or against, the Castro government in Cuba. In spite of that fact, we had operated a large, four-engine aircraft in and out of Ft. Lauderdale without once being questioned. We often speculated on how "the word" is passed from one government agency to another when the one is engaged in activities the other is responsible for preventing.

I drove to Miami next day with Eric and checked into the Gateway Motel. The other men followed later. Phil turned in the rental car and by six o'clock we were all packed into one room, burning furniture with cigarettes and squabbling over one bottle of Scotch and four glasses. Eric said that we should eat if we were hungry because we would not be departing until much later, and we wouldn't have another opportunity until some time the next morning. We had rustled up more glasses and another bottle of Scotch, so no one was interested in solid food except Gordon. He left and came back with two multi-deck hamburgers.

Eric returned at 7:30. He told us to leave the room two at a time at two-minute intervals, walk up 34th Street, turn right at the end of the block, and get into a panel truck that was parked a few yards up the street. The truck was a Hertz van without windows. Two wooden benches were attached to the walls inside. Eric said not to talk and not to make any noise. He closed the doors and we drove through the city for 30 minutes.

At first the sounds of heavy traffic on the streets and the constant stopping and starting at traffic lights identified our route as through the downtown business section of Miami. Then came long stretches of uninterrupted, traffic-free progress. We tried to plot our course by keeping track of turns and timing the intervals between stops. By the time we slowed for a final turn into what was obviously a gravel driveway, no one had the slightest idea what part of the city we were in. We all gave Ferd the Navigator hell.

Eric opened the doors and we climbed out into the fresh air. The truck was parked on a circular driveway in front of a vintage southern mansion with squatty columns supporting a roof that covered a porch across the entire width of the house. The porch was brightly lighted. The light spilled out onto the driveway and faded out through the trees down in the direction of a highway. The house was set well back on a large lot and was out of sight from the road. Eric said to "just hang around outside for a few minutes," and he and the driver disappeared through the front door. We waited for an hour and a half. There were no signs of life in the house. A light burned in the front hall but no lights showed through any of the windows which were all heavily curtained. Finally Eric reappeared and said, "all right gentlemen, let's go." We got back into the truck for another 40-minute drive. There was no explanation for the diversion to the old house.

We drove back through downtown Miami, again identified by traffic sounds. Leo had just begun to curse "those stupid GI bastards" when the truck slowed, made a sharp turn, and came to a complete stop. We heard the sound of voices outside. After a short wait, the truck proceeded in low gear for a short distance before coming to another stop. Then we heard the familiar sound of a hangar door being opened. The truck moved ahead and the hangar doors closed behind us. Eric opened the doors, and we stepped down onto the floor of a large, empty hangar. We were parked beside a door that led into what had been a parts shop. Shelves and bins still lined the walls. Some of them held suitcases and other gear. Blackout curtains covered the windows inside the office. There were a couple of couches against a wall. In the middle of the room was a card table covered with magazines and dog-eared paperbacks. A few straight-backed chairs were scattered around the room. Over in one corner a stocky, bald man dressed in a T-shirt and shorts sat behind an old wooden desk. Eric introduced him as "Nick."

"At least it isn't Jim," Gordon muttered.

"Well, gentlemen," Eric said, "I'll leave you here. Nick will give you your further instructions." That was the last we saw of Eric except for a brief encounter many weeks later when Gordon and I flew the "mutineers" into Homestead Air Force Base from Nicaragua.

"I'm glad we're rid of that pontifical, GI bastard," Leo said.

Leo was a chronic malcontent, but at times he did manage a well-turned phrase.

Nick was businesslike and not overly communicative. He told us to tag our suitcases and "stow our gear" in one of the bins along the wall. We were instructed to take everything out of our billfolds except money and our phony papers and stow them, too. Then Nick checked over the things in our duffle bags to make sure all identifying labels had been removed.

"Just make yourselves at home," he said when we had finished. We learned later that Nick was a Lieutenant Commander in the U.S. Navy.

We waited for an hour. Sandy went to sleep and began to snore. He started softly, then built up to a crescendo, at which point he woke himself up. During one of these lulls, Leo pulled his chair up close to Sandy.

"Do you know what I'm going to do with you when we get down into the jungle?" Leo asked.

"What are you talking about, Leo? Gowan. Let me sleep."

"I'm going to take you out in the woods one night, you hairy bastard, and tie you up in the top of a tree. Then I'm going to sit back and watch to see what comes up after you."

"I know what it'll be," Gordon said, "a big, fat lady gorilla."

Nick came in from outside. "All right, fellas, You can board your aircraft now. It's on the ramp at the far end of the hangar. Don't show any lights on the ramp."

We waited for another hour in the airplane. Two men came in and went forward to the cockpit. We heard them talking in a foreign language — not Spanish. This was our first contact with the so-called "contract crews." They were a group of pilots who, as we learned later, had come over from somewhere in Southeast Asia. They were in an entirely different category from our group. Their flying activities were confined to flights between Miami and Central America to transport Cuban recruits and supplies to the training bases. There were five or six of these "contract" pilots. I believe that at least two of them were Polish.

We heard small scuffling sounds outside on the ramp. Another man came on board wearing a pistol on his belt. He came forward in the cabin and spoke to us briefly.

"We are taking some Cubans down with us," he said. I have instructed them not to move around and not to try to come forward into the cockpit area. I suggest that you men get yourselves as comfortably situated as possible and stay put throughout the flight. We'll be about six hours. I will be up forward. If there is any trouble, I'll come back and take care of it."

He walked back and stood by the large loading door at the rear of the cabin. Forty Cubans came up the ladder and filed into the aircraft. They were uniformed in stiff new fatigues (right off some supply sergeant's shelf, no doubt). They were of all ages from 20 on up. Some looked to be in their late 40s. Most of the older men looked soft and out of shape. They had all obviously come directly from some recruiting and supply depot in the Miami area.

The men in our group had taken seats well forward in the cabin. They were long, canvas, bench-type seats that ran the length of each side of the cabin. The empty deck was a heavy, metal cargo floor with tie-down rings spaced at intervals. There was not enough room for everyone on the canvas seats. Some of the Cubans stretched out on the cargo floor. They looked at us with curiosity and apprehension. They hadn't expected us any more than we had expected them.

It occurred to me that the man up forward with the pistol probably had a valid reason to be on board. His reference to "trouble" was possibly more meaningful than we had at first understood. With thousands of Cubans seeking sanctuary in Miami every month, it would be unrealistic to assume that some Castro agents and informers were not among them. It would be equally unrealistic to assume that one or more of these might not be among us at the moment, on board the aircraft. To commandeer a C-54 load of anti–Castro rebels, along with a mixed bag of CIA pilots, would be a neat trick to pull off. It would earn someone a lot of brownie points back home in Havana. I began to look our Cuban passengers over very carefully, but I couldn't find a face that looked as if it belonged to a Castro infiltrator; or perhaps I should say they *all* looked that way.

My inspection of the Cubans was interrupted by the hum of an inverter followed by the cranking of the number three engine. In a minute all four engines were running and the aircraft began to move forward. I could tell by the amount of power the pilot used to get underway that we were heavily loaded. I sweated out the takeoff. We must have used at least five thousand feet of runway before we were airborne. I mentally checked off all power adjustments, and when we were well established in a climb, I settled back and returned to my inspection of the Cubans.

After an hour or so in flight it began to get cold in the cabin. I crawled under the long seat, pulled a jacket over my shoulders and went to sleep on the deck, fenced in by a row of boots, and with the posterior of the man above me about three inches from my face.

I slept for several hours. When I woke up it was apparent that the sun was high in the sky, even though its light was filtered through the aircraft's heavily painted windows. I worked my way out from under the seat, trying not to step in anyone's face in the process. A cigarette sliced the gloom at the far end of the cabin where two Cubans were talking and waving their arms around. Somewhere back in the same direction Sandy's dulcet tones were audible above the sound of the four engines. Gordon was on the floor, sitting with his back to the door of the cockpit. His knees were doubled up under his chin and he had both arms wrapped around his shins. Gordon's eyes were wide open, unblinking, and fixed on something somewhere in distant space. I leaned over and asked him if he were alive.

"No," he said.

Phil had fallen over sideways in the seat. He looked bad. His face was puffy and showed the strain of chasing the belly dancer for three weeks. I leaned across Phil and put my eye to a scratch in the pane on one of the windows. Below was an unbroken expanse of jungle. By working my eye around to a different angle I was able to see a towering mountain peak just ahead and to the right of our course. I signalled this intelligence to Gordon by making a pointing motion downward with my finger. At that moment the pilot reduced power. The break in engine rhythm roused the sleeping men. They began to untangle themselves, and the cabin became a bedlam of Spanish.

There were more power reductions. As we lost altitude, the air became heavy and hot. By sound alone I was able to follow through on the approach — flaps down, gear down, a turn on final, followed by more flaps. After we had touched down, and had slowed sufficiently, we turned off the runway. Almost immediately we made a turn back parallel to the runway, taxied a few feet and stopped. The pilot shut down the engines. I was puzzled. We couldn't be more than a few feet off the runway. We were not. The clearance between the runway and the taxi strip and ramp at Retalhuleu could almost have been measured with a yardstick. Aircraft taking off and landing at Retalhuleu had only a few feet of clearance from the wing tips of aircraft parked on the ramp. The "ramp" was really nothing more than a wide space in the taxi strip. In practice, as it turned out, this didn't become the mental hazard that might have been expected. The narrow runway provided only four feet of clearance on each side of the aircraft's main gear. The concentration required to keep the aircraft in the center of the runway eliminated any concern we might have had about the proximity to the parked aircraft.

The man with the pistol came out of the cockpit, walked back to the door and pushed it open. The Cubans all filed down the ladder first. We could hear shouts of greeting as they were recognized by friends who had preceded them to Retalhuleu.

Central America

I was the first of our group down the ladder onto the ramp at Retalhuleu. The heat was so intense and the humidity was so high that stepping onto the ramp was like stepping into a sauna. Before I could adjust my eyes to the heat and glare, a hand was on my arm and a voice said, "I need a pilot this afternoon, Buck. Are you ready — after you eat?"

It was Hal McGee.

"You're kidding of course, Hal. You've got to be — aren't you?"

"Not if you feel up to it," Hal said. (He didn't wait for me to say whether I felt up to it or not.) "Get one of the other pilots and you all take a load over for us this afternoon. We haven't had any C-54 pilots and we need to get going in a hurry. The aircraft's all loaded. Go eat — and I guess you'd better find some bedding and a bunk. You won't be back until late tonight."

The rest of the crew had disembarked and were listening to our conversation. Their relief that they had not been first down the ladder was apparent. I asked Gordon and Leo to go with me. Gordon staggered away groaning, and Leo spat viciously toward the wheel of the aircraft.

Hal led us toward the two-story frame building at the edge of the ramp. It looked as if it had been originally intended as an airport terminal. There was a small structure on top that probably had been designed as a control tower. Inside, just to the right of the entrance from the ramp, two steps led down into a dining area. Along one side of this room cafeteria facilities were set up. Behind the counters a door led into a kitchen. Eight tables were set up in the middle of the dining room. They were picnic-type tables with backless wooden benches attached on each side. In the center of each table there was a cluster of salt and pepper shakers, a bowl of sugar, bottle of catsup, jar of mustard and about a thousand flies.

The natural heat of the day, along with the heat from the kitchen, and a pervasive effluvia of something cooking, combined to produce one of the most effective appetite deterrents I have ever encountered.

There was only one man in the mess hall — Bill Peterson. There was a plate of something in front of him which I failed to recognize even when I sat down at the table directly across from him.

"Ugh," he said.

"Bill," I said, "is that a word of greeting for an old pal, or is there something you're trying to tell me? What is that you've got there on that plate?"

"Dead goat."

"It doesn't exactly make my mouth water, Bill. How is goat prepared in this restaurant?"

"They kill him."

"Hal says you're going to ride with us this afternoon and show us the way to Tide." (Tide was the code name for Puerto Cabezas. Retalhuleu was Mad.)

"Aren't you going to eat some goat first?"

"Isn't there something else — something I could sort of train on?"

"Yes. They've got chicken."

"Maybe I'll try the chicken."

"Have you seen any of the chickens down here? They're made entirely out of feathers and skin and bones. You'd better have the goat."

I decided to wait until starvation was well advanced before attempting any of the local cuisine.

I had only a short time to learn something about the base before leaving on my first flight to Puerto Cabezas. The main building served as base headquarters. In addition to the kitchen and mess hall, it provided administrative personnel with living quarters and offices. It was by no means a large building and it had not been designed for anything approaching the utilization it ultimately achieved.

Over the mess hall and kitchen, a mezzanine had been inserted between the ground floor and the one above it. Throughout the building, partitions had been erected whenever the need arose to make two, three, and even four rooms out of one. Since the number of cubic feet of space available was limited, space to partition became progressively harder to come by. One cubicle had just been fabricated on a landing between the first and second floors. It was just large enough to hold one small folding cot, which seemed to be occupied day and night. It was a "private" room only in the sense that it could be occupied by only one man at a time. I assume not by the same individual. By the time I arrived at Retalhuleu the headquarters building looked like the inside of a hive of drunken bees combined with some of the features of a "crazy house" at an amusement park.

The small frame structure on the roof of the building was in use as living quarters for the B-26 pilots who had preceded us to Retalhuleu. Predictably, it was referred to as the penthouse. The penthouse was constructed of unfinished lumber. Two-by-fours supported a plank roof covered with tar paper. The tar paper absorbed the heat of the sun and transferred it with undiminished intensity to the area below. Pine boards, nailed to the supporting two-by-four columns, extended halfway to the roof. The remaining space was screened. The occupants of the penthouse basted in their own sweat day and night except when frequent tropical thunderstorms at night swept through the screen on 50-knot gusts of wind. Access to the penthouse was through a door on the second floor and up a ramp to the roof.

I staked out a lower bunk in one of five double-deck bunks spaced around the sides of the penthouse. Pete Ray, Bill Peterson, Don Gordon and Joe Hinkle were already in residence. Al Walters and Ron Smith had moved to Puerto Cabezas. Riley Shamburger was also at Puerto Cabezas. Hal McGee was at Retalhuleu and lived somewhere in the "beehive" below us. Ernie King, Phil Chapman, Gordon Neilson and Sandy Sanders took over the remaining bunks in the penthouse. Red Cornish, Jack Vernon, Wade Gray and Fred Ealey established themselves in one of the barracks behind the administration building. Ferd Magellan flew over to Puerto Cabezas with me that first day and remained there.

I had a good view of the entire base from the penthouse. The one runway ran northwest and southeast. Not only was it barely wide enough to accommodate a C-54, the runway had a slight crown in it to provide an additional challenge; and at 4,800 feet, with temperatures in the 90s, it would have been illegal back home for a C-54 at gross weight. There was no "go, no-go" decision to worry about. If an engine failed on takeoff, the runway was not long enough to continue on three engines, nor was it long enough to get the aircraft stopped before plunging through the fence and down the hill at the far end of the field. As we used to say, the "go, no-go" decision was made when we left the penthouse. The southeast end of the runway was 150 feet higher than the opposite end, enough of a grade to make it necessary to take off downhill and land uphill.

Aircraft were parked on the taxi strip *cum* ramp. They were lined up nose to tail like elephants in a circus. Sometimes there were as many as six in the line. There was no way to turn an aircraft around or to move it in any direction except straight forward. Guerrillas unfriendly to President Ydigoras would only have had to slash the tires on the aircraft in front of the line to immobilize all the rest. (These guerrilla bands were considered a perpetual threat to the air base.)

The administration building was located near midfield. It was so close to the parking ramp that a good broad jumper could have made it from the roof of the building to the tip of the wing. Two typical army-type frame barracks were located behind the administration building. Each barracks was furnished with rows of double-deck bunks, and occupied by 20 to 30 men.

In line with the barracks was an assortment of smaller buildings used to store supplies for the base and for aircraft maintenance and repair. Maintenance on the aircraft was performed outside on the ramp.

At the far end of this row of miscellaneous buildings a small, one-room structure served as a "club." Club facilities were limited. There was one large table, a half-dozen chairs, a bar hammered together from scrap lumber, and no ice. The club was open 24 hours a day and in use by from one to thirty men at any given moment.

Well beyond the end of the runway at the southeast end of the field, there was another group of barracks. They were separated from our complex by, maybe, a half-mile. These buildings were occupied by a detachment of Guatemalan troops stationed on the field, so we were told, to protect the base from attack from the communist guerrillas stooging around in the mountains to the east. (Apparently there have *always* been communist guerrillas stirring up trouble throughout Central America.) How effective these troops may have been in the event of an attack on our base, was very questionable in my own mind. I watched a company at target practice one morning in the field directly back of our building. They were firing at targets set up at a distance of not more than a hundred yards. As far as I could tell, from the puffs of dirt kicked up in the general vicinity of the targets, not one of them ever hit a target. Firing at an enemy, it didn't look as if they could have come close enough to make him flinch. I couldn't bring myself to watch this performance for more than a few minutes. It may be that some of them eventually found the range. I doubt it.

The air base at Retalhuleu was located on a strip of land approximately one-and-a-half miles long by a half-mile wide. A six-foot-high fence made of corrugated metal siding blocked the field from the view of anyone traveling on the highway that paralleled the field on the west side. It blocked the view, that is, if everyone kept traveling. Anyone who stopped, and everyone did, to look through the wide spaces between the sheets of siding, could get a full view of the base. The east side of the field was bordered by a simple barbed wire fence that also closed in both ends of the field. The railroad from Tapachula to Guatemala City and San José ran along the edge of the field just outside the fence. Two trains a day went by pulling ten or 12 cars with people hanging out of all the windows, and standing between the cars. The base and all of the aircraft and associated activities were in full view of the passengers on these trains. We often stood on the roof outside the penthouse to wave to them. They always waved back.

I took off on my first flight to Puerto Cabezas about two hours after we arrived in Retalhuleu from Miami. Hal handed me the necessary navigation charts with the courses to be followed marked in red pencil. It was not a simple matter of taking off from Retalhuleu and heading directly across the mountains to Puerto Cabezas. Such a course would have carried us over El Salvador and Honduras. We were not permitted to enter the airspace over those countries. Instead, we turned southeast after takeoff, crossed the port city of San José, and continued out to sea for 25 miles.

Then we took up a southeast heading and flew parallel to the coastline until we were opposite the Gulf of Fonseca which washes the shores of three countries — El Salvador, Honduras and Nicaragua.

At the Gulf of Fonseca we turned and flew east-northeast across Nicaragua to Puerto Cabezas on the Caribbean Sea. On the final leg across Nicaragua we had to fly at an altitude of 11,000 feet across the mountains before dropping down over the jungles and the coastal plains. The return flight followed the same courses in reverse. It was a three-and-a-half to four-hour flight each way.

Gordon, Leo and I discovered immediately that our airlift responsibilities involved a whole series of "dicey" operational challenges. To begin with, we were numbed by the sight that greeted us when we climbed the ladder into the aircraft. The entire cargo area was piled high with boxes of ammunition. To reach the cockpit we had to go on hands and knees through the space between the boxes and the roof of the aircraft. There was a manifest and a weight and balance sheet on the pilot's seat. These alleged that the weight of the aircraft and cargo was 73,000 pounds. This is the exact maximum gross weight for a C-54. I judged this to be the sole basis for the manifest and the computations on the weight and balance chart. In the weeks ahead, our aircraft *always* weighed exactly 73,000 pounds.

Hal had told us to refuel at Puerto Cabezas, and he told us what quantity of fuel to take on. The practice, we learned, was to carry only enough gas for the round trip between the two bases. The result was that we always left Retalhuleu with just enough fuel to make it to Puerto Cabezas — provided, of course, that we always hit Puerto Cabezas right on the nose.

It was necessary to sacrifice excess fuel for payload. This was fine, except on dark nights when the weather was bad over the mountains, or Puerto Cabezas was blanketed by low clouds, or someone had forgotten to turn on the homing beacon at Puerto Cabezas. All or some combination of these problems invariably prevailed.

When we made our way forward, we found the cockpit of the C-54 like the inside of a pressure cooker. In a matter of seconds we were all soaked with sweat. It poured off my forehead into my eyes. I had to tie a handkerchief around my head in order to see. Sweat ran down my arms and dripped off the ends of my fingers. My hands were so slippery I couldn't get a firm grip on the control column. Like a Mack truck, a C-54 requires a good grip on the wheel, and a good bit of muscle to boot.

"Let's get this thing in the air," Gordon said. "I think I'm going to faint."

Leo got the four engines running and we went through the first checklist. When I advanced the throttles to start taxiing, I knew something was wrong.

"Having a little trouble getting underway, Captain?" Bill Peterson was leering over my shoulder.

"Very funny," I said. "This thing was either loaded by saboteurs or it's stuck in the asphalt — or both."

Normally, 800 rpm's is a good power setting to taxi a C-54. At 800 rpm's this aircraft didn't budge. I advanced the throttles. Still no sign of life. I pushed the throttles up over halfway. The aircraft began to inch forward, with shrill, metallic squeals of protest coming from somewhere down in the neighborhood of the landing gear.

We waddled out to the end of the runway, the aircraft squealing all the way. I expected the gear to fold any second. We went through the takeoff checklist. I looked down the length of the runway, and gave some thought to turning in my resignation. That was the shortest 4,800 feet I had ever faced. I turned to Leo who was sitting on the jump seat between me and Gordon.

"Look, Leo, keep your eyes glued to those engine gauges. If anything goes wrong, don't wait for me or Gordon to call the engine. *Feather* it. But don't feather as long as we're pulling any power at all. Okay?"

"Okay, Cap'n, but it really won't make any difference. This sonofabitch is never going to get off the ground."

"Let's try to think positively, Leo."

"Let's taxi this thing back to the ramp and think positively about heading back to Birmingham," Gordon said.

With my left hand on the nose steering wheel, I advanced the throttles to 30 inches of manifold pressure. Gordon followed on through to 56 inches with the throttles on his side. The aircraft accelerated unbelievably slowly. In fact, "accelerate" is not an accurate word to describe our performance in the first 1,000 feet of runway. I moved my hand from the nose steering column at 70 miles per hour. I didn't look at the airspeed indicator again. There was no point in looking. Three-fourths of the runway was behind us. There was no stopping now, and when we reached the end of the runway we would either fly or go chugging right along through the cotton gin at the foot of the hill off the end of the runway. Actually, I believe we crossed the boundary without altering our trajectory, and became airborne only when the ground dropped away into the shallow valley at the end of the field. Leo raised the gear without waiting for me to call for it, and we gained enough airspeed to avoid the cotton gin. Leo milked the flaps up and things seemed to go a little better. We probably had all of five hundred feet when we crossed the coastline and headed out to sea.

For a start, we leveled off at 5,000 feet and flew parallel to the coast about 30 miles offshore. Gordon assumed his fixed, unblinking, straight-ahead stare. Leo immersed himself in a paperback book with a naked girl on the cover and the words "Sex Kitten" in the title. Bill fiddled around at the navigator's station back of the pilots' seats. I played with the automatic pilot for a while and managed to get us locked in on what seemed to be a reasonably good heading to make landfall at the Gulf of Fonseca. Then I fiddled with the radar. There was no weather, but I wanted to compare the radar representations with actual coastline terrain features and with the chart of that area. In the absence of adequate radio navigation facilities, radar would become a principal navigation aid, and we were also able to use the radar to create reasonably precise instrument approach procedures.

Far below us was a tiny splinter on the ocean, a ship making her way north with a "bone in her teeth." Almost 30 years earlier, working as a deckhand, I had been on such a ship in that same location off the coast of El Salvador, heading north to San Francisco, and then on to China.

I went to sea at 17 on a four-month voyage from New York to China and return. The agreement I had with my parents (I thought of it as a kind of loose understanding) was that at the end of the voyage I would return home and go back to school.

On its return, our ship remained in its home port of Brooklyn for only seven days. Before anyone could get a rope on me, I was gone again. I would probably still be gone if my father hadn't been waiting on the dock for me at the end of the second voyage.

I was beginning to get hooked on something as firmly as a drug addict gets hooked on dope. Going to sea gets into some people's blood. So does flying an airplane. Like booze or narcotics, I think, it's a form of escape. In flight or at sea, you become conscious of the distances that separate you from all the overcrowded shores beyond the horizon. The sense of isolation is pervasive, but for many, it brings with it a feeling of comfort and security, not despair.

For more than 3,000 years, whenever the tide was right and the weather was good enough to make it out of the harbor, men have been hauling up sails, and putting out to sea. But, somehow, I don't believe that the men who sailed with Leif Ericson cared whether he discovered Newfoundland or not. And I don't think the men who sailed with Ferdinand Magellan cared if the earth was round or square. I think mostly they just wanted to get out to sea. The airplane opened up a new dimension to be explored by the spiritual heirs of the Phoenician, Viking, and Portuguese seamen who began the job of cutting the earth down to size.

Flying down the west coat of Central America, the air was unbelievably (to me) clear. The sky was deep blue, washed here and there with brush strokes of white. From our altitude the sea was a vast expanse of blues and greens in random patterns that blended in the distance with the horizon. Off to the east, towering, snow-capped peaks grew right up out of the sea.

To the captain of the ship plowing north below me, these mountains, clearly visible from his bridge on a day like this, are accurate position checkpoints, just as they are to me. We each have charts on which coastline features, the mountain range, and individual peaks are accurately located. Over land, or sea, or in the air, there is no better way for a navigator to locate his position than by reference to some clearly identifiable terrain feature.

Accurate navigation is essential if you travel through the air or across the sea. Navigating on land from one point to another is simply a matter of staying on your own side of the road, paying attention to highway signs, and not going to sleep at the wheel. In the air, or at sea, there is no physical track that connects point A with point B. The track is only a line drawn on a chart. The direction of the track is a compass heading. Even if you are able to hold this heading exactly, there are always ocean currents or winds aloft to push you off to one side or the other. So unless you know where and how much to compensate, holding a heading out of A won't get you to B, but somewhere on one side or the other, or before or beyond.

It is easy to understand the superstitions and terrors that have filled the minds of sailors through the ages. Tossed around like chips on the face of a sea that extended to the edges of the earth, they sailed for months without knowing where they would make landfall, or if they would be able to find their way back home. With the primitive knowledge and tools they used for navigation, the wonder is that they ever ventured out of sight of land.

National Geographic once published a photograph of two sets of footprints laid down in Africa about a million years ago, covered and preserved through the ages by a thick layer of volcanic ash. The footprints were made by a male and female (man and wife?) — prehistoric ancestors of *Homo sapiens.* The tracks extend for only a few hundred yards, then disappear in a vast African plain in the direction of a range of hills in the distance. It doesn't take a lot of imagination to picture a couple of our prehuman ancestors setting out one morning to discover what that distant range of mountains might have to offer. Maybe things were getting a little too crowded back at the cave. Maybe it was just curiosity. Whatever it was that inspired that man and woman a million years ago to strike out across that vast and inhospitable plain has become for modern man a kind of genetic inheritance. All through recorded history (and obviously before) people have been striking out for parts unknown.

The greatest obstacle to early exploration was not a lack of nerve. It was not the difficulty of crossing rivers and climbing high mountains. It was not even the terrors of the unknown seas. The greatest obstacle was navigation — how to find the way from point A to point B, and back. Science and technology have taken most of the guesswork out of navigation today. Navigation signals are transmitted from satellites; inertial navigation systems that need no signals have been invented; radio transmitters cover the earth with a network of airways. All are coupled to computers which are in turn coupled to automatic steering devices that will fly an airplane or sail a ship, leaving the modern navigator with little more to do than punch a couple of numbers on a keyboard before getting his aircraft or ship (or even submarine) underway. For thousands of years, however, well up into the present century, navigation has depended on a familiarity with celestial bodies, prevailing winds, and ocean currents to steer an accurate course. Herdsmen and travelers in the desert used the stars and prevailing winds for direction. The Polynesians learned to identify wave patterns to navigate between the islands of the South Seas. Some mariners took birds along to point the direction of the nearest land. The art of cartography was born and navigators began to chart coastlines and to plot significant landmarks on their charts. Lighthouses were constructed, identified by smoke during the day and by bonfires at night. As the sea lanes became more heavily traveled, more and more detail was added to maps. Astronomers and mathematicians prepared tables to show the declination of stars at various times. A primitive kind of celestial navigation began to develop. Mariners ventured farther out to sea for longer periods of time. The ancient Phoenicians sailed through the Pillars of Hercules and north to the British Islands and the tin mines of Wales. Vikings crossed the north Atlantic to Iceland, Greenland, and the continent of North America. In 1492 Christopher Columbus made landfall in the Bahamas after two months at sea. The ships of Ferdinand Magellan sailed into South Hampton after a two-year circumnavigation of the earth.

The invention of the quadrant, followed by the sextant, then the octant made pinpoint (comparatively speaking) accuracy in navigation possible. A good navigator can take up his octant, pick three stars and shoot them, and within a few minutes fix his position within a radius of ten miles. He can, that is, if he is on a ship at sea moving along at 10 to 25 knots. The airborne navigator, because he is moving at far greater speeds, is seldom as sure of where he is as where he was 100 miles back. If the skies are obscured throughout the hours of darkness, it doesn't matter much to the ship's navigator. His ship will only advance 150 to 200 miles during the night. In only five hours in flight, however, an aircraft may travel well over 1,000 miles, which creates a different problem for the airborne navigator. One way or another, in a short period of time, he must identify his landfall and put into harbor. Unlike the ship at sea, he can't heave to and wait for daylight. So, without the stars, or the sun and moon, or radio navigation aids, the aircraft pilot/navigator is reduced to very much the same limited capabilities of Columbus when he crossed the Atlantic 400 years ago — dead reckoning. In Central America, particularly at night, our navigation was often reduced to the same primitive techniques.

Dead reckoning is simply the process of keeping track of how fast you are going, in what direction, and of changes to other speeds and directions. It means plotting periodic positions on a chart as you go, and being able to deduce the net results of the various changes in direction and speed into a specific position for any moment in time. Four hundred years ago the speed of a ship at sea was measured by heaving a small log overboard attached to a long line with knots tied in it every 50 feet. The log was allowed to drift aft for 30 seconds while someone counted the number of knots paid out over the rail. This equalled the number of nautical miles (knots) per hour the ship was making good. When a pilot refers to how much time he has "logged," or to his "log" book, he may not know it, but that's where the expression originated.

At speeds computed with the log, Columbus and his contemporaries plotted all the zigs and zags of heading changes on a chart. By "deduced reckoning" these could be converted into a position at the end of the day. It wasn't highly accurate, of course, but it was in the ballpark. The term "deduced reckoning" was shortened to "ded. reckoning" which was later converted by some navigator with a macabre sense of humor to "dead" reckoning. Today that term has been shortened even more to simply "DR."

In principle, DR navigation is exactly the same in an aircraft as on a ship at sea, the *big* difference being that time in flight is measured in minutes, not in hours and days. Accurate airspeed indicators and accurate gyroscopic heading indicators produce much more accurate navigational results than were possible for Christopher Columbus *provided* that the pilot holds steady on his headings, and keeps accurate track of his time and airspeed.

Pilotage is a navigation technique more applicable to aircraft than to ships at sea, except back in the days when ships stayed in sight of land and fixed their positions by reference to known landmarks on shore. Pilotage is simplest in fair weather when visibility is good; more difficult in poor weather and at night, and impossible over the open sea and above clouds.

Pilotage involves laying out a track on your chart, determining the track's compass heading, and then following it from the air. You fix your position as you go by identifying prominent landmarks along the track. If, for instance, on your original heading, flying at 175 miles per hour, you *should* have been directly over a particular lake in 30 minutes but, in fact, in 30 minutes you identify the lake ten miles ahead and ten miles off to your right, it is obvious that your progress has been affected by a head wind blowing from your right. You estimate the correction necessary to put you back on your track, and to hold you there once reestablished. If you are flying any considerable distance, your progress will be marked by a constant series of such heading corrections as wind velocities and directions change.

At first, finding your way across country from a mile or two high in the sky is confusing and frustrating. From the air the earth is like a huge patchwork quilt of open fields and forests, mountain ranges, scattered lakes and ponds, crisscrossing rivers, highways and railroads, and small villages, towns and large cities scattered across the landscape at random. This is a panoramic view. At first you don't see all the small details. With practice you learn to see this panorama as a huge chart unwinding off a giant roller on the horizon ahead of you, moving slowly rearward below your wings. The multicolored chart on your lap is a smaller version of this big picture, and you learn to match the sawmills, golf courses, major highways, river bridges and dams with the identical features displayed on your chart.

Unfortunately, pilotage and DR are already becoming lost arts. Even small trainers today are equipped with radio navigation systems that require of the pilot only that he be able to tune a frequency, center a needle by turning a small knob on a bearing selector, and keep it centered with whatever small heading corrections may be necessary. When a small flag on this instrument flops from "to" to "from" he knows that he has arrived over the station the radio is tuned to. There is no need for him to look outside the aircraft en route, and, for the most part, many newly trained pilots today seldom do. However, if he has made no effort to combine pilotage with radio navigation, and the radio fails, this pilot may have to land somewhere to find out where he is.

As we cruised at 5,000 feet down the coast of El Salvador on our first flight from Retalhuleu, I switched the radar to the mapping mode and set it on a 100-mile range. The radar showed a perfect picture of the coastline off to the east. We were 35 miles out at sea. Ninety miles ahead, the radar displayed a clear outline of the Gulf of Fonseca where we would alter course and fly east across Nicaragua. I was greatly relieved. A good radar would solve many navigation problems in a part of the world where radio navigation aids were few and far between, and what there were worked only intermittently.

Bill came forward from the navigator's station to fill me and Gordon in on what had happened to the B-26 pilots since we parted in Miami.

Most of the B-26 pilots' time in Retalhuleu had been spent instructing Cuban pilots in formation flying and gunnery. Many of the Cubans had limited or no experience as military pilots. Some were short on experience of any kind. The most glaring weakness was in aerial gunnery. As Bill put it, "When we got down here most of the guys couldn't hit the side of a barn. Some of them couldn't even hit the pasture the barn was standing in."

The Cubans had constructed a target of bamboo poles, pine boards, and some 50-gallon drums which they set afloat in a small lake a few miles inland from Retalhuleu. Every day the Cuban pilots attacked the target with six 50-calibre machine guns installed in the nose of each B-26. (This is enough concentrated fire power to knock a steam engine sideways off its tracks.) When Bill and the other pilots arrived, the target was still afloat. The Birmingham pilots destroyed it the first time out.

In the few weeks before we arrived from Ft. Lauderdale, the B-26 contingent put in many productive hours with the Cubans. Some of them also checked out on C-46s. The C-46 is a twin-engine transport similar to, but much larger than, the C-47 (DC-3). Our B-26 pilots also learned about the staging base at Puerto Cabezas. Some of them assisted in an initial airlift of supplies and equipment from Retalhuleu to Puerto Cabezas. They were confined to the base. They could only fly a couple of hours a day, and they found that time dragged. However, there were a few incidents that broke the monotony.

Joe Hinkle and Al Walters were assigned a mission one day to fly a C-46 to a small, private grass airfield in the interior of Guatemala. They had to slow the aircraft down and drag it in over the tops of some palm trees growing at the approach end of the field. A wing tip clipped the top of one of the trees, and the C-46 wound up in a ball half in and half out of the woods at the far end of the field. The aircraft was totaled. Miraculously, Joe and Al got out without a scratch. Sadly, a Guatemalan native who was picking coconuts in the top of the tree they hit was killed.

One morning a truckload of Cubans from the training camp in the mountains was taken for a swim on a beach close to San José. Four of the men were attacked and killed by sharks. By coincidence, Don Gordon was overhead in a B-26 at the time of the attack. His attention was attracted by the truck and the group of men on a stretch of beach that was normally deserted. Flying low over the water for a closer look, he found himself a horrified and helpless witness to the last, desperate moments of the four swimmers as they fought the sharks. He watched as a pack of sharks churned the sea to blood and foam.

Great excitement occurred one afternoon when a lone B-25 appeared over the field. It circled several times at an altitude of three or four thousand feet. It gave no indication of an intention to land. Some of the Cuban pilots quickly identified the B-25 as one of Castro's aircraft. Bill Peterson was the only pilot in the air at the time and he was in a B-26 many miles south. Bill was contacted by radio and instructed to head for Retalhuleu and attempt to intercept the B-25. Two B-26s on the field were cranked up, but as soon as they started to taxi toward the end of the runway, the B-25 headed east and disappeared over the mountains.

On another occasion a large delegation of press representatives from the United States and Latin American countries visited the base. The afternoon before the delegation arrived on the base, our pilots loaded every aircraft with all the Americans and Cubans on the base and flew down to an airfield near San José. They laid low through the night and the next day while the press was conducted on a guided tour of an air base that was manned exclusively by Guatemalan forces.

On April 9, Paul Kennedy, a correspondent for the *New York Times*, was kicked out of Guatemala by President Ydigoras. Kennedy was based in Mexico City. In January he had filed a story from Guatemala describing the air base at Retalhuleu and the training camps in the mountains. In fact, due to a lapse in security, he penetrated two miles beyond a checkpoint which was as far as outside observers were permitted to proceed. He saw large numbers of military personnel in training, but he failed to identify them as Cubans.

Kennedy described the air base at Retalhuleu quite accurately, and he said that it did not appear to be suitable as a major air force installation because of a lack of dispersed hardstands and taxiing facilities. In this he was entirely correct. Overall, Kennedy's story tended to confirm, rather than to refute, the Guatemalan government's position that the military activity at the air base and in the training camps was a response to a threat of hostilities with Cuba. Kennedy said that military personnel were in the area in force, and were being used as instructors. He also said that United States funds were being used to finance the operation.

In response to the story Kennedy filed in January, the Guatemalan newspaper *Diario de Centro Americo* had said, "Mr. Kennedy is an inaccurate reporter, a liar, and an imposter." Kennedy had seen more than he should. Therefore, when he showed up in Guatemala again in April, he was summoned to national police headquarters (a week before the first air attack on Cuba) and given a message from President Ydigoras that he was to pack up and leave the country immediately. To explain Kennedy's expulsion, the President's press secretary, Augusto Mulet said, "Kennedy was in Guatemala some months ago and telephoned his newspaper lying reports that in Guatemala foreigners were being trained to invade Cuba."

Paul Kennedy was on top of a story but he just didn't quite get it. It is fascinating to be in a position, as I was, to observe and to follow the day to day efforts of the news media to uncover information, and the concomitant efforts of the various governments involved to keep the lid on.

When we made the turn at the Gulf of Fonseca, I pushed the props and throttles forward to climb power, and we began a slow climb to 11,000 feet. We crossed the coast and were soon over forbidding terrain so completely blanketed by the jungle that solid ground was only visible where mountain tops broke through the restraining cover. There were occasional, isolated clearings where aboriginal inhabitants had carved out small patches of community life.

It isn't always easy to relate to what you see of the world from the air. Those places on the earth's surface from which you depart in an aircraft, and those places to which you return, have been especially prepared for you. Everything in between is inherently hostile — even when you are flying over your own real estate. What was below us now was definitely not our own real estate, and it was hostile. One would survive a crash landing here only to find one's head being shrunk over a fire on the end of a sharp stick. Over the rain forests of Central America, four engines is not enough. But then, neither would six, or eight, be enough.

As we approached the east coast of Nicaragua the terrain became less forbidding. The mountain range and the heavily forested foothills were far behind. Soon we were over the coastal plains. We established a slow descent and altered course to hit the coast south of Puerto Cabezas. I was acutely aware of the lack of radio navigation facilities along our route of flight. It was obvious that at night, or on instruments, there would be no way to make course corrections by reference to any identifiable terrain features or relative bearings off radio signals. Campfires of savages are not good checkpoints, and along the coastlines human habitation is concentrated in widely scattered villages which, without lights, are unidentifiable from the air at night.

I set the radar on the 25-mile range and tilted the antenna down so that it would paint the coastline as we flew north toward Puerto Cabezas. I wanted to check the radar display with the actual terrain and also against the chart. I felt certain that there would be times when the only way I would be able to find Puerto Cabezas was by radar, and there were no alternate airports within fuel range. I was able to locate the position of the field when we were about ten miles south. Two small lakes a couple of miles southwest of the runway, and a long pier extending out into the Gulf less than a half-mile south of the runway were easily identifiable on the radar screen.

"That's going to be a lifesaver," Gordon said. He had been observing the radar closely as we were inbound to the field. "You can turn to zero-nine-zero a couple of miles south of that pier, go out for two minutes, make a one-eighty, and you'll be on final for two-seven, or enter downwind for nine."

Gordon was right, and we subsequently used that approach procedure several times. It worked out quite well.

The runway at Puerto Cabezas was longer and wider than the runway at Retalhuleu. It was laid out east and west. Since prevailing winds were almost always from offshore, takeoffs and landings were usually made to the east.

As I crossed the field and turned downwind, I observed that the south side of the runway was lined up for almost half its length with B-26s. They made up quite an impressive armada. There was a long, frame building, a shed with a roof but no sides, on the north side of the runway adjacent to a paved ramp. There were two small structures beyond the east end of the runway, but I couldn't find anything to indicate that a large complement of men was located anywhere on the field. As I turned in on final at about 600 feet, however, I caught sight of a small, square water tower poking out of the trees only a few hundred feet south of the approach end of the runway. A closer look revealed a sizeable tent camp well hidden in the trees.

A jeep drove out to the runway and directed us to the ramp by the long shed. Under the roof of the shed there were large numbers of crates and boxes of ammunition piled in high stacks. The load we had brought over was added to the inventory.

Ron Smith and Al Walters were in the jeep. We shook hands. They wanted to know how long we had been at "Mad." "Mad" and "Tide" were code names we used for Retalhuleu and Puerto Cabezas. They asked us how we liked it over there.

We said we had arrived only two hours before our departure and had not had time to draw any conclusions, but when we did, we didn't think they would be too favorable. We asked Ron and Al what was going on at Tide and how they liked living in tents. Al said they didn't know what was going on, and that they didn't think much of Tide, although the tents were better than the penthouse. There was plenty of beer but no whiskey, nothing but cheap, local rum. Al said the rum tasted like molasses that had been spiked. He said food was not bad, but tarantulas and scorpions made life miserable. One man had been stung by a scorpion and had to be flown back to Miami for treatment. Ron said that he had been trying to find a scorpion to bite him so that he could get a trip back to Miami. Spiders and scorpions had discovered that they could stay warm and comfortable at night down inside a boot, so it was dangerous to put your boots on in the morning without shaking them out good first.

Plumbing facilities at Tide were primitive. A six-hole privy provided one accommodation. A 14-foot section of water pipe with holes bored in it at intervals served as the camp shower. The pipe was installed over wooden flooring that had been laid on the ground directly opposite the mess tent. The flow of water through this pipe was controlled by a valve at the water tower. It was turned on for one hour twice a day—from 11 to 12 noon, and from six to seven in the evening. Water trickled from the holes in the pipe in pencil-thin streams spaced about two feet apart. Each hole in the pipe represented a "shower" position. To take a bath, you found an unoccupied hole, lathered up, and hoped that you could rinse off before someone cut off the flow of water. A big man, thoroughly lathered, had to work fast.

To complicate matters even more was a very small snake, indigenous to that part of the world, whose venom was said to be so poisonous that if you were bitten, you would be dead before you hit the ground. I saw a lot of men in the shower with their boots on—including me.

At midday as well as in the evening, shower time coincided with meal-time. You could take your choice. You could take a shower and watch other men eating in the mess tent, or you could eat and watch other men bathe. If the latter was not the most appetizing arrangement, it was at least edifying.

A pump and filter were used to transfer water from a stream to the water tower. The water tower supplied the camp with water for cooking, drinking and bathing. Mostly, people drank beer and Cokes. Because of the poisonous snakes, tarantulas and scorpions, and the uncertainties of timing a shower with the water supply, bathing was not a number one priority. In the crowded mess tent, people were always trying to get upwind from each other.

Twelve-man tents were pitched under the trees in rows that ran at right angles to a company "street." The street was a ten-feet-wide area that had been stripped of trees and undergrowth. It started up near the end of the runway and ran down through the trees to a point close to the small stream where the water tower was erected.

A typical army field kitchen was installed in a tent that blocked the far end of the company steret. Next to it was the first aid tent where Doc Barr lived and performed his services. Next to Doc's tent was the mess tent where everyone ate whatever they thought they could stomach after picking it up in a chow line at the kitchen. At the far end of the company street, near the end of the runway, another "street" angled off into the trees. Here there were a number of frame shacks that housed radio and instrument repair shops, an ordinance shop, and a general supply shop. As at Retalhuleu, air-craft maintenance and repairs were performed outside on the line.

The tents that served as living quarters were all set up on the south side of the company street. The tent that I eventually moved into was at the end of the street closest to the runway. The Cubans who had already moved from Retalhuleu lived in tents at the far end of the camp.

One group of tents and three small frame buildings were located in the center of the camp. They were separated from surrounding tents by a bar-rier of accordian-type barbed wire — the kind used to protect trenches and gun implacements on a battlefield. All the camp brass lived in this com-pound. An armed guard was on 24-hour duty at the entrance. The largest of the three buildings in the compound served as an operations head-quarters. The other two buildings housed administrative and security per-sonnel, and communications equipment, including the "long line" to Washington.

As we were getting ready to leave the flight line, Al said that Reid Doster was expected in that afternoon. He had hardly gotten the words out of his mouth when a flight of B-26s came roaring in overhead from the north. The formation broke left and landed. We drove in the jeep to where the lead aircraft was parking, and waited for Reid to shut down. Reid got in the jeep with us and we drove down the runway to the camp.

No one knew (or would say), including Reid Doster, how close we were to D-day. But the transition from Retalhuleu to Puerto Cabezas was in steady progress. Already there were more people in camp at Tide than were left at Mad. Reid told us that he had made his last trip back to the States and that he would remain in camp until the mission had been completed, whenever that might be.

Cuban aircrews, the "foreign nationals" we had heard about back in Birmingham, were already in camp. They had been briefed, or, at least, partially briefed. In any event, they were completely sequestered and their movements were highly restricted. They were even required to fall in and be marched in formation to the six-hole accommodation. It is hard to imagine anything less conducive to regularity.

Our job in the weeks ahead was to complete the airlift of equipment, supplies, and personnel from Guatemala to Nicaragua. We would have very little time to talk to anyone but each other, to learn anything about the "big picture," or to do anything but eat, sleep and fly. Soon we established living quarters in both camps. Often, when roused for a flight, it took a few minutes to decide which side we were on — not that it made any difference.

Against headwinds, the flight back to Mad on our first round trip took four hours. We took off from Tide at 10:30 that night. The interior of Central America is unbelievably dark at night. Even in the most thinly populated areas of the United States, lighted villages and towns cover the landscape, and in thickly populated areas around large cities the landscape is ablaze with multicolored, pulsating, and flashing lights. Flying across Nicaragua at night, even though safely encapsulated in the 20th century, you are suspended in darkness two miles above a primeval terrain where an occasional pinprick of bright orange marks the place where Stone Age man lies sleeping beside his spear. You can almost believe that the jungle around him crawls with life forms that have elsewhere long since passed from the face of the earth.

Gordon nods in the seat beside me. Bill and Leo are asleep in the two bunks in the companionway. The even, steady sound of the four engines is occasionally broken by a rhythmic beat when one of the props gets out of synchronization with the others. A slight pressure on the prop controls eliminates the beat. Otherwise, I sit unmoving in the cockpit with my eyes fixed on the curtain of stars that hangs between me and the distant rim of the earth. There must be a million more stars in the clear night sky over Nicaragua than I have ever seen back home. I am acutely conscious of what lies in the darkness below. An eerie feeling grows that we, in our aircraft, have become subjects of some sort of time warp, fixing us on a thin boundary between time periods separated by thousands of years.

Over the Pacific coastline we turn and fly northwest for an hour, then begin a long, gradual descent. We identify the city of San José and turn inland toward Retalhuleu. A faint, flashing beacon in the distance identifies the field at Mad, but when we arrive overhead there are no runway lights. We have to circle the field for 20 minutes before someone comes out in a jeep to put flare-pots alongside the runway. We can see the headlights of the jeep moving slowly down the runway. A flare appears first on one side, then on the other. Two or three flares on the approach end of the runway are all we need. I start our final approach before the jeep has worked its way more than a quarter of the length of the runway. I turn on final and line up with the two or three flares in place, hoping that the driver of the jeep will know that we intend to land and will get off the runway. Leo hits the light switches and the landing lights come on sweeping forward in two white arcs. We continue our approach. The landing lights find a runway between the flare pots. The headlights of the jeep race down the runway and turn off at the administration building.

When we taxi to the ramp, the jeep is parked and the driver has disappeared. A Guatemalan sentry is stretched out on a wooden bench under a mango tree. He is awake, but ignores us as we file wearily up the walk from the ramp into the darkened building. It is three o'clock in the morning when we fall into our bunks in the penthouse. It is almost 48 hours since we have been to bed. I promise myself that I will sleep until noon, but I am awake at nine o'clock in the morning, soaked in sweat. The temperature in the penthouse is already in the 90s.

In the weeks following our arrival at Mad we were engaged in a grueling schedule of almost daily flights between Guatemala and Nicaragua. We usually left Mad in the afternoon and returned in the early hours of the next morning. We flew as a crew of two pilots and a flight engineer. Gordon, Leo Baker and I worked things out where we usually flew together as a crew. We slept when we could, sometimes at Mad, sometimes at Tide, and often in flight in one of the bunks in the aircraft. Because our flight schedules seldom coincided with camp routine on either side, our meals were often baloney and cheese sandwiches eaten in flight.

We used our infrequent days off to take care of things like laundry, letters to the folks at home (which arrived with postmarks from a variety of widely scattered places in the United States), and we sometimes joined in what seemed to be an ongoing effort to lower the liquor level in Guatemala by a foot or two. The club bar was a 24-hour-a-day operation to accommodate a variety of work schedules.

In Birmingham and Florida our contacts with representatives of the company were limited to one or two people at a time. In Birmingham we had met briefly with Al, Frank, Jake and Hoyt. We never saw Jake or Hoyt afterwards. Al and Frank were in Retalhuleu and, later, in Puerto Cabezas.

Both were in positions of high authority, although we never did figure out who was superior to whom.

In Ft. Lauderdale Eric was our principal contact, and Mac was our instructor in recurrent training on the C-54. Gordon and I saw Eric again at Homestead Air Force Base the night we flew the mutineers in from Tide. We often saw Mac at both Mad and Tide. He flew regularly between Florida and the two bases. Mac had some kind of responsibility for the "contract" pilots.

In contrast to these earlier contacts, we were in close daily contact with company personnel at Mad and Tide. By "close" I don't mean that we did business regularly or had personal dealings with everyone in both camps, but we did all live together in our restricted surroundings. We drank beer at the camp bars, and pitched darts or horseshoes with whoever happened to be available. Everyone knew everyone else, but on a first name basis only. Everyone did *not* know what everyone else's duties and responsibilities were. This was not necessarily a deliberately contrived state of affairs, but was more a product of the unusual work schedules of the pilots and other crew members. So, except for the men who were our active, working superiors in the flying department, we had little opportunity to learn what anyone else did, where he stood in the table of organization, or what his rank and branch of service was back in the States. The fact that an individual appeared to us to have some comparatively minor function, did not mean that he might not be a high ranking officer in one of the military services. For instance, on my first afternoon at Tide I drew bed sheets, towels and a bar of soap from a somewhat elderly gentleman who, I learned later, was a retired Air Force Brigadier General. I doubt very much if he was in Guatemala for the sole purpose of handing out bars of soap to pilots.

The Birmingham airmen's immediate superiors were Vic and Connie. They were both pilots, and they were permanent employees of the company or one of its established proprietaries. As such they were distinguished from people like Eric and Mac who were regular Air Force officers on detached duty with the company, or like Reid Doster who was on temporary leave from his Air Guard unit, or like us who had been hired under contract to do a specific job.

Vic and Connie were subordinate to Larry. Larry was not a pilot, but as time went on it became apparent that he stood at the top of the pecking order. I met Larry the day after I returned from my first flight to Tide. I was at the club in the afternoon watching some men pitch horseshoes. A C-46 appeared at the far end of the field flying at about 800 feet. The aircraft made one pass down the length of the field, circled and came back on another pass. On the first pass, I saw a man standing in the open door of the aircraft. Someone said Larry and some airborne troops were going to jump. I didn't know who Larry was, but on the second pass he did jump, followed by some 30 Cubans. They landed in the area between the barracks and the perimeter fence. It was a good drop considering the restrictions of the drop zone. The Cubans were picked up and carried away in a truck. In about 15 minutes Larry came wandering into the club. I assumed that he was an instructor for the Cubans' parachute force. He turned out to be the head honcho in the field. I don't know why Larry was jumping with the Cubans—maybe just to keep his hand in.

Larry was a tall man in his mid-forties. He was quiet and low key in words and behavior. Like Vic and Connie (and Frank) he was a permanent company employee. He obviously had a substantial military background. Al and Frank were in charge at Tide until Larry moved over from Mad. All three were superior to General Doster. Doster's personal presence in the operation was not required by the company. His area of expertise was reconnaissance, not ground support. The 117th Recon Wing of the Alabama Air Guard had had recent experience with B-26s. The company needed the Wing's enlisted specialists in engineering, maintenance and repair, ordnance, armament and the other technical skills required to provide ground support for our B-26s. The company also needed General Doster's support and cooperation. To get this, they took him along in the deal. He was a great favorite with the Cuban airmen, and he accomplished a lot in maintaining their morale.

If all this sounds like a confusing and inefficient chain of command, it was not. The fact is, there was no particular reason for us to know the precise place where everyone fit in the chain. There was no compelling reason, nor any great interest, in sorting everyone out into their respective branches of the military or company service as long as we knew from whom to take our orders, and there was never any question about that. The point is (a point that seems to have been lost in most of the critiques of the Bay of Pigs), the leadership was highly professional.

Transition flights between Retalhuleu and Puerto Cabezas stepped up considerably during the first week in April. An increasing number of flights between the two bases moved the last of the materiel and personnel from Mad to Tide. On one of these final flights my cargo was aluminum outboard motor boats.

Don Gordon and Ernie King made a flight to Miami to pick up Miro Cardona who came to Retalhuleu to speak to the Cubans and to tour their training camps. I'm sure it was a flight Mr. Cardona will not forget. Don said that the return flight from Miami, late at night, was through an almost unbroken line of thunderstorms. Although he may not be aware of it, this flight came close to being Mr. Cardona's last. Ernie misjudged his position and began a descent over Guatemala much too early. They broke out into the clear momentarily, just long enough for Don to spot a 13,000-foot peak directly ahead. Don said that he had just time to grab the control column, bank steeply, and pull up sharply, back into the overcast. He said that they missed crashing into the mountain peak by what he judged to be a matter of feet. They climbed to 15,000 feet and stayed there until they passed over the radio beacon at San José and could let down safely out to sea, which is what they should have done to begin with.

Pilots of ships and aircraft are often challenged by the awesome forces of nature in line squalls and thunderstorms. Bad weather is the pilot's worst enemy, and it must be avoided at all costs when it is possible to do so. It is not always possible, of course. Pilots have an old adage that flying is hours of boredom punctuated by moments of sheer terror. There is nothing more terrifying than a pilot's view ahead of a sky boiling with black clouds that are bombarding each other and the earth below with bolts of lightning.

Winds inside a thunderstorm can build up to fearsome velocities, and they move vertically as well as horizontally. At one minute you can be going up like an elevator at more than 2,000 feet per minute. In an instant you can start down the other way just as fast. Once I entered a thunderstorm at 5,000 feet. Five minutes later I was spat out the side of the thunderhead, like a watermelon seed, at 16,000 feet.

The impact of rain (which you're praying won't turn into hail) against the windshield only a few inches in front of your face is deafening. Often it is impossible to hear radio signals and communications. The lightning is blinding. The buffeting can become so severe that even your safety harness can't protect you from banging up against the roof and the sides of the cockpit. Often you emerge from these contests looking as if you had been in a fight — and you have.

It is essential to maintain control of the aircraft in these situations. There is nothing to show you what the aircraft is doing, or rather, what is being done to it, but a panel full of instruments vibrating so badly that they are almost impossible to read and, more importantly, to interpret. Nowhere else that I know of can you be made more aware of your own insignificance and the pitiful frailty of your craft than in the center of a storm.

At moments like these — the "moments of sheer terror" pilots speak of — there are psychological factors that must be dealt with as well as the purely physical and mechanical. You can think about the awesome forces of nature exploding all around you; you can think about towering peaks and rocky gorges below you; you can worry about whether the cargo is securely tied down in the cabin behind you; you can agonize over the thought of running into ice, or hail the size of golf balls. You can think about all of these things if you want to, or if you can't help it, but it won't do you a bit of good. All you can do is sit there and take it, try to stay in control and, above all, to maintain your composure, for if you lose your "cool," you will probably lose the battle, no matter how good a pilot you may be.

Man was designed as a dry land animal. On the water, under the water, or in the air, he is out of his natural element. It is only because of the intellectual gifts with which he was endowed that man was able to design and fabricate a variety of craft to transport him out of his natural element, and because of an unbridled imagination, coupled with a compelling curiosity, that he was inspired to use them.

Even so, in spite of all the technological accomplishments that have made modern ships and aircraft virtually accident-proof, there are many people who cannot bring themselves to venture out onto the sea or into the air. I suspect that much seasickness results not so much from the motion of the ship as it does from the sight of all that water and the knowledge that the nearest land is a couple of thousand feet straight down.

There are many people who have never been in an airplane, and who have no intention of ever getting in one. Fear of flying is sufficiently widespread that it is a clinically recognized phobia. Fear, of course, is a natural instinct. You come into the world with fear already programmed in — or you should. Fear is an instinctive reaction to danger. All animals, including the human species, must be able to sense danger in order to survive. A person without fear is a person without imagination. He has not been properly programmed for survival. He cannot project the possible consequences of his actions, or of his failure to act. He does not recognize life-threatening situations. Most people are able to control their fear with varying degrees of success. A complete loss of control, however, results in panic, which only compounds the danger that inspired it.

If a pilot cannot accommodate to, and eliminate, the psychological pressures of functioning in a dimension that he was not intended by nature to occupy, then in moments of stress his performance will be seriously impaired. He must learn to perceive of himself as a kind of extension of the aircraft, as another integral component, so to speak, because the aircraft *is* designed to function in that dimension.

Oddly enough, there are active, working, professional pilots who suffer from a fear of flying, some even to an excessive degree. What motivates them is not any particular love for the sky and flying, but rather a compelling desire to *be* a pilot — as distinguished from a desire to engage in the specific activities required. The most irrational manifestation of this syndrome I have encountered was in a pilot I once knew who always preferred to fly at 1,500 or 2,000 feet rather than going on up to 10,000 or 15,000 feet where the air was smooth and, sometimes, the winds were advantageous. I could never get him to explain this aberration, and it took me a long time to figure it out for myself. This pilot suffered from a fear of flying. He didn't want to get any farther away from mother earth than he had to. The closer he was to the ground, therefore, the better he liked it, even though the results of an engine or structural failure at 1,500 feet were no less conclusive than at 15,000. Presumably, the only time he was completely comfortable in an airplane was when it was parked on the ramp.

I became persuaded that Phil Chapman was of this genre. I flew with Phil on his first flight to Tide. He was in the left seat. As always, the aircraft was well over gross. At the prescribed climb power setting we were getting nowhere fast. We would have been halfway to Tide before we reached our final altitude of 11,000 feet. Phil started cursing the aircraft, "this sonofabitch won't climb," etc. That's *all* he did. After wallowing around like a stricken whale for 20 or 30 minutes, I increased the power to the maximum allowable continuous power setting (META). Phil began to curse the amount of fuel we were using at META. I pointed out that we would burn far less fuel at META for 20 minutes than we would at climb power for an hour. Phil opined that "we must be way to hell over gross." I agreed. Phil cursed the people who had loaded the aircraft. He was working himself into a real tizzy and we hadn't even leveled off at altitude yet.

There was a strong southerly wind blowing. It kept pushing us closer to the coastline than we were supposed to fly. Phil would let the aircraft drift to within five miles of the coastline, then make an exaggerated correction to take us back out to sea. We zigzagged like this all the way down to our turning point at the Gulf of Fonseca without ever having an opportunity to pin down the wind velocity and direction. Phil cursed the wind.

When we were about an hour out of Tide, it became apparent that the radio beacon was not in operation at the field. Phil had been holding a heading that was unlikely to compensate for the strong southerly wind that was blowing, which at this point we were only able to guess at. A good guess was that we were well north of our track, however. We were above broken clouds, but it wouldn't have made any difference if the night had been clear. There are no checkpoints over the middle of Nicaragua in the middle of the night — only those scattered Indian campfires.

Without the radio beacon to guide us directly to the field, we would have to guess when we hit the coast if we were north or south of Puerto Cabezas. If we guessed wrong, we would turn the wrong way and be flying away from Puerto Cabezas instead of toward it. We could easily run ourselves out of gas before we figured out what had happened and reversed course. Because of the heavy cargo load carried on the flights to Tide, we never had enough gas to spare for unnecessary milling around trying to find the field. Phil was now cursing the radio and the Nicaraguan Air Force people who were responsible for the beacon.

"Phil," I said, "turn right 20 degrees."

"Twenty degrees right?" Phil was almost screaming. "Jesus Christ, we're not going to *Panama*. Look at those goddamn fuel gauges."

"Phil," I said, "turn 20 degrees right and quit worrying about Panama. We have to be certain we are south of the field when we hit the coast. That way we'll be certain which way we have to turn. My guess is that with the wind we've had, we'll only be a few minutes south of the field. Now go ahead, turn right 20 degrees."

For the first time, Phil got the picture. He continued to curse the aircraft, the amount of fuel we were limited to, the winds aloft, everyone connected with the mission, and, incredibly, even the *sheets* he had been issued for his bunk back at Retalhuleu. To cap it all off, Phil was at least 1,000 feet too high on his first approach. We would never have gotten on the ground — at least not with the runway under the wheels.

On his second try, Phil established an approach speed on final that might have been okay if we were empty and light. At our weight the approach speed was far too slow. The aircraft felt as if it were going to fall out from under us, which it was. You could feel it in every nerve and muscle. Phil didn't feel anything. I asked him to let me handle the power while he concentrated on flying the airplane. I added power. I kept on adding power. We crossed the end of the runway at almost full throttle. It was a mess.

Phil's agitation began the moment we climbed on board the aircraft back at Mad. His agitation continued to grow throughout the flight. It was out of all proportion to anything that was actually happening. He made a basket case out of himself for no reason at all. I knew that the last place in the world Phil had any business being was flying an old C-54 around at night in Central America (or anywhere else for that matter). He knew it too. More than that, the last place *I* wanted to be was sharing responsibilities with the possessor of a psychological profile I had learned to recognize long ago.

Gordon also made one flight with Phil. Gordon wasn't into psychology. To him Phil simply became "that bastard." Gordon and I worked things out so that on most future flights we flew together, with Leo, leaving Ernie to cope with Phil and Pithecanthropus Erectus.

Everything began to point to a fast-approaching D-day. Hal McGee, Vic, Connie and Larry had all moved over to Tide. All of the B-26 pilots except Don had long since moved out of Mad. Mac arrived on one of his periodic flights from Miami during the night of April 7. I found him comfortably ensconced at the club when I came in on a flight from Tide at six o'clock in the morning on April 8. Mac said that he was staying to help fly the troops over to the other side. Later that day, and on the next day, C-54s flown by the "contract" crews began to arrive at Mad.

By mid-afternoon on April 9, there were six C-54s and three C-46s lined up on the narrow taxi strip and ramp. Late that same afternoon Larry and Frank came in from Tide. They said that the Cubans would begin to come down from their camp in the mountains the next night. We would fly them to Nicaragua during the night where they would immediately board ships lying just offshore at Puerto Cabezas.

That night we all took sidearms to bed with us — except Phil. Phil drew a Thompson submachine gun. None of us had much faith in the ability of our Guatemalan guards to hold off a determined attack by guerrillas. The threat was quite real, although none of us had paid much attention to all the rumors that had been floating around about guerrilla activities back in the hills. President Ydigoras's expressed fears of an attack by Fidel Castro were, of course, spurious. However, he did have reason to be worried about the ambitions of former President Arbenz who was supported by the Castro government in his effort to regain power.

If the Arbenz guerrillas planned a raid, this would be the ideal time for it. The long line of transport planes at the field provided ample evidence that the long anticipated movement of the Cuban invasion force was imminent. If they could get past the government troops, all the guerrillas had to do was disable the first aircraft in line, and all the others would be unable to move, which would leave all of us pretty well trapped.

On the way up to bed in the penthouse later that night, I stumbled over a prone figure on the roof. I reached for the .45 on my belt.

"Goddamnit, Buck, can't you see?"

It was Phil, complete with Tommy gun and a couple of drums of ammunition.

"What the hell do you think you're doing, Phil? I almost plugged you."

"I'm spending the night right here," Phil said. "Those bastards can get over the fence easy, before that bunch of Boy Scouts down at the end of the field even know what's happening. Do you realize what kind of shape we're in here? You better get your gun and come out here with me. We can take turns sleeping."

"I've already got my gun," I said. "In fact, I almost shot you with it. I'm going to hit that sack, and I advise you to do the same thing."

"Not me, buddy. There's no way those guerrillas won't make a try tonight. Do you think they don't know what's going on? Look at that goddam ramp. Covered up with airplanes."

"Listen," I said. "If anybody gets past the Guatemalans, we've had it — unless we can slip away in the dark. I was nervous enough to begin with. Now I'm twice as nervous with you out here with that gat. You'll either shoot your own head off, or plug some Guatemalan guard patrolling the fence. Come on in here and let somebody else worry about the guerrillas."

Phil struggled to his feet. "Okay. But just *remember* about three o'clock in the morning that I *told* you guys."

As we entered the penthouse a voice from Leo's bunk said, "Thank God for small favors. Now we can all get some sleep."

"How would you like to go to hell, Leo," Phil said.

An hour after dark on the night of April 10, a long convoy of trucks entered the base at Retalhuleu. Cuban Brigade 2506 began to board the aircraft that would transport them on the first leg of their journey to the Bay of Pigs.

Throughout the entire period when we were flying day and night in Central America, newspapers in the United States continued to report "invasion" activities in Florida and Guatemala. No one discovered the most important installation, the base at Puerto Cabezas.

Accusations and recriminations between irate governments continued to fill the air. Propaganda campaigns were stepped up by all sides. Guatemala's Ambassador to the United States, Carlos Alejos, said, "...Cuban leaders are megalomaniacal puppets." Alejos also said that every statement by leaders in Cuba that invasion forces were being trained in Guatemala "is an outright lie," and that Cuban charges reflected only resentment over Havana's repeated failure to overthrow the Guatemalan government. Alejos said that "the current training of Guatemalan troops is not secret and is purely defensive."

(Carlos' brother, Roberto Alejos, owned the land on which the Cuban training camps had been established, and the property on which the air base at Retalhuleu had been constructed.)

On March 22, the choice of Miro Cardona as president of the new Cuban "Revolutionary Council" was announced in New York. Asked whether the revolutionary group had received moral or financial help from the United States, Cardona said, "Definitely no."

On April 3, the U.S. State Department issued a pamphlet that had been prepared by President Kennedy, Arthur Schlesinger and Richard Goodwin. After summarizing the history of the Castro revolution, the pamphlet concluded: "We call once again on the Castro regime to sever its links with the international communist movement, to return to the original purposes which brought so many gallant men together in the Sierra Maestra and to restore the integrity of the Cuban revolution.

"If this call is unheeded, we are confident that the Cuban people, with their passion for liberty, will continue to strive for a free Cuba; that they will return to the splendid vision of inter-American unity and progress; and that in the spirit of José Martí, they will join hands with other republics in the hemisphere in the struggle to win freedom."

Newspaper reporters had not been idle during this period. Miro Cardona's tour of the Guatemalan training camps in April was reported in the *New York Times*, as were the heavy purchases of medical supplies and blood plasma in Miami by Cuban doctors.

On the night of October 11, we flew the last of the Cuban brigade from Retalhuleu to Puerto Cabezas. I never returned to Mad. I assume that it reverted to exclusive use and occupancy of the Guatemalan military, no doubt to the vast relief of President Ydigoras and his government.

The C-54 crews had gone to work almost within a matter of hours after arriving at Retalhuleu. Before their arrival, most flying activities had come to a halt. Consequently, unlike the B-26 pilots in our contingent who had had considerable contact with the Cubans, we had almost none. I had no idea how many Cuban pilots were at the base, and I did not know what their role was to be in the forthcoming invasion. I was aware of what we had been told at our briefings in Birmingham, that we, B-26 and C-54 pilots alike, would be engaged in the first combat missions against Cuba.

There was never any conscious judgment on our part that this constituted an indictment of the Cubans' courage, motivation, or dedication to their cause. Having little contact with the Cuban pilots, we were largely unaware of their frustrations and the animosity that had developed between the Cubans and the Americans.

The Cubans who arrived in Guatemala, either as ground forces or as air forces, arrived there only after first making successful escapes from their own country. Usually this was accomplished at great personal risk and sacrifice to themselves and their families.

Many of the Cuban aircrews had been in Guatemala for several months before we arrived. They were men who had been members of the Cuban military air forces, or pilots for one or another of the two Cuban commercial airlines.

No doubt those who had been in military service in Cuba found it easier to adjust to circumstances in Guatemala than it was for people like Captain Eddie Ferrer and others who had flown for the Cuban airlines.

Captain Ferrer had gotten out of Cuba by hijacking his aircraft on a regularly scheduled flight, and flying it to Miami. This was not easily accomplished. An armed guard was stationed on every scheduled flight for the express purpose of preventing just such a hijacking, either by passengers or the crew. To make good his escape, Eddie Ferrer had to enlist the help of coconspirators (in itself a risky business in Havana in those days) and take the plane at gunpoint.

Ferrer found himself "on the beach" in Miami with only five dollars in his pocket. Within a matter of hours, however, he was able to locate pilots who had preceded him to Miami. Within a matter of only a few weeks, he and other pilots, after intensive screening, were enlisted in the organized efforts being sponsored and managed by the company.

Ferrer and his group were flown to San José in Guatemala. They arrived in September 1960. Construction work at the air base in Retalhuleu had not been completed. They were loaded on trucks at San José and driven to a coffee plantation in the foothills. Conditions there were miserable. Their barracks was a large storage barn. Each man was issued a standard GI stick-and-canvas folding cot, and a mess kit. The "mess hall" was a flat, concrete slab outside the barn normally used for drying coffee beans. The men lined up for their meals at a typical GI field kitchen where typical GI fare was slopped into their mess kits.

There was no privacy, and there was no plumbing. The men bathed in a pool, shaved in a trough, and took care of their other needs in a doorless, three-hole privy. It was not unusual for a pilot to be joined in the privy by an Indian lady plantation employee who would plop down beside him with a friendly smile and a pleasant "good morning."

The men were instructed in basic close-order drill, and they were put to work unloading trucks that arrived daily with supplies destined for use by the ground forces of the Cuban brigade. That the pilots should become discouraged and unhappy in these circumstances is understandable. They were compelled to subordinate themselves to their U.S. "advisers" to an extent where often it appeared to them that they were merely military hired hands in someone else's army, rather than principals in their own war of liberation. In many respects, this was quite true.

To anyone who has served any time in basic military training, all of this is easily recognizable as standard GI operating procedure. To former officers and airline pilots like Eddie Ferrer, worried about families left behind in Cuba, concerned for the future of their country, and denied a part, or any information, involving the planning and organization of their efforts, these early days must have been traumatic—added to which was the indignity of all pilots, anywhere, who are forced to engage in the kind of foot-soldier work they were put to. Pilots expect to fly. Any other activity is viewed as a waste of time.

After two weeks at the coffee plantation, the Cuban pilots were moved to the air base. Living accommodations and other amenities were a vast improvement over primitive conditions at the plantation. A 4,800-foot paved runway had been completed. Standard military barracks, warehouses, repair and supply shops, and a combination administrative-headquarters building contributed to an environment the Cuban aircrews could more easily relate to.

There was indoor plumbing and a kitchen and dining area. Unfortunately, a Guatemalan caretaker force had not yet been screened and trained. For another short period the Cuban pilots were required to do KP, wait on tables, scrub floors and clean latrines.

Eddie Ferrer says, "We were dumbfounded and humiliated to find that we had suddenly become servants as well as officers."

A feeling of strain and bitterness continued to develop in relations between the Cuban pilots and their United States advisers.

Flight training began shortly after the Cubans moved to the air base. Vic and Connie, the two company pilots, were their principal instructors. During this early training period four aircraft were destroyed in training accidents. In October a drop mission was flown to supply guerrillas operating in the Escambray Mountains north of Trinidad on Cuba's south coast. The C-54 was hit by antiaircraft fire over Cuba, knocking out one engine. On the return flight the plane ran into bad weather. The crew made an emergency landing in Mexico near the Guatemalan border. The Mexican government confiscated the aircraft, but released the crew. The Cuban Liberation Air Force had lost five aircraft in a matter of a few weeks.

In his written account of his experiences, Captain Ferrer says: "Rayo (Retalhuleu) Base presented many challenges, not the least of which was the resolution of cultural clashes between the Americans and the Cubans. In our situation, it was critical that a working relationship based on respect and friendship be established. Unfortunately, several events precluded the formation of such a relationship."

One of the events alluded to by Ferrer involved the construction of the "Club." The Cubans watched as the building went up, unaware of what purpose it would serve. When it was completed, the final touch was added. The sign over the door read CLUB, and in smaller print, "Authorized Personnel Only."

As far as the Cubans were concerned, it might as well have read "Americans Only." No Cuban was admitted unless invited by an American and this happened rarely. A great deal of bitterness resulted from the building of the club.

Eddie Ferrer, and presumably other Cubans, interpreted this as a "lack of respect and friendship." The Cubans' sensitivity was, perhaps, understandable. However, they did not correctly understand or interpret their fundamental relationship to the American advisers, nor did they fully grasp their respective roles and responsibilities in the overall operation.

As far as "friendship" was concerned, the Cubans should not have expected a lot of good fellowship and fraternization. That they were excluded from much that they believed they should not have been, was a function of maintaining absolutely essential security. For instance, the location of the staging base at Puerto Cabezas was a tightly guarded secret. Puerto Cabezas was well within range of Castro's aircraft. For Castro to learn of the existence and location of this base could have had serious consequences. Company personnel could not run the risk of having conversations among themselves in the club overheard by anyone who did not need to know. It was not a question of trusting or not trusting the Cubans. It was simply a matter of preventing any possibility, however remote it might have been, of compromising the mission. Our group was also excluded from knowing about a lot of things unless, or until, it became necessary.

The Cubans, who were so sensitive on this subject, might be surprised to know that company personnel do not even talk to each other unless all parties to a conversation happen to be engaged in an activity together. Many of the Cuban pilots had worn military uniforms, but none had ever really been engaged in a wartime military operation. If they had, they would have understood the situation in Central America better. As it was, they believed that they were being discriminated against as "Cubans" instead of as people who had no "need to know."

An illustration of the soundness of this policy can be found in the resignation of 12 pilots in the Cubans' Liberation Air Force. In December, these men, for one reason or another, had become discouraged, dissatisfied and disgruntled. Among the 12 who quit and returned to Miami were the second in command of the entire unit, the C-54 squadron commander, and the C-46 squadron commander.

Eddie Ferrer "found it difficult to believe that our comrades would give up the privilege of fighting for their country." With more experience, Eddie would have known that in these situations, there are always some who will "give up." And you never know who they will be until you get there. Company personnel understood all this quite well, and it was their responsibility to ensure that anyone who *might* quit did not leave camp and return to Miami with a lot of information that could easily fall into the hands of Castro. They were not there to demonstrate what "good guys" they were. In any event, none of us, including the Cubans, had come to the God-forsaken boondocks of Central America for a picnic.

As for "respect," it did not come automatically with the job. When the Cubans earned the respect of their American supervisors, they got it — wholeheartedly. Interestingly enough, among the most highly respected of all the Cubans who participated in the invasion was Captain Eddie Ferrer himself.

Another aspect of the situation that the Cubans may have failed to understand was the motivation of the American pilots. Today in Miami there is a monument inscribed with the names of all the men who lost their lives in the effort to liberate their country. Inscribed in a place of honor are the names of the four Americans who were shot down at the Bay of Pigs. It is an honor for these men to be included with the Cuban heroes, but what the Cubans may not have grasped, as they should have, is that the Americans, all of us in one capacity or another, were fighting for the United States. To us the liberation of Cuba was incidental to that purpose. To the Cubans, quite naturally, it was paramount.

We were not mercenaries or soldiers of fortune who sell their services for any cause to whoever will pay the most. We were employed by our own government to fight for our own country in the same way the Cubans were fighting for theirs.

Bay of Pigs

I made four flights from Retalhuleu to Puerto Cabezas on Monday and Tuesday, April 10 and 11. Leo Baker flew as flight engineer, and "Ray," the company pilot who had been recognized by Earl back in Ft. Lauderdale, was in the right seat. He had shown up in camp a couple of days earlier, along with a number of other extra pilots, to help out in the massive airlift in progress.

The United States military instructors who had trained the Cuban brigade accompanied them on the trucks that brought them down from their training camps to the air base. Some of the leave-takings were emotional. There was a lot of embracing, backslapping, imprecations to "give 'em hell," and vows to meet again soon in Havana. Later on, after the invasion was over, I wondered if some of the Cubans at squad and platoon leader levels — having been cast ashore, so to speak, at the Bay of Pigs — may not have suffered to some extent from the lack of accustomed leadership by these men who had guided them through their entire training.

The thing that impressed me most about the individual members of the brigade was that each man was armed with an automatic weapon and carried a portable radio transceiver. If necessary, each individual soldier was equipped to shift into a guerrilla mode well armed and able to establish and maintain communications with others. This was a contingency always clearly recognized in the original planning.

It was well after midnight when we landed on our last flight into Puerto Cabezas. We were guided off the runway onto the ramp at midfield. The area was crowded with company personnel and Cubans. They were all milling around in the lights of a half-dozen trucks lined up alongside the ramp. The men we had brought over moved directly from the aircraft to the trucks, which were quickly filled. The company people mounted jeeps and took off down the runway in the direction of town and the harbor. They were followed by the trucks. In a few minutes Leo and I were left standing on the dark ramp beside the aircraft. Ray had disappeared. The two of us walked in silence along the deserted field toward the camp. A long row of B-26s was in the darkness along the far side of the runway.

As we passed, we could see clusters of rockets mounted under the wings of the aircraft.

Most of the tents were dark when we entered camp. Halfway down the company street a light burned outside the entrance to the compound, and lights were on in the operations and communications shacks just inside the gate. A few people were milling around at the far end of the street by the mess tent. We found Riley Shamburger, Vic and Connie hunched over cups of coffee.

"Well, I see you lucked out again," Riley said.

"I think we just brought in the last bunch," I said. "Will we be going back over?"

Riley raised his eyebrows at Vic.

"That's your last trip for awhile, Buck. A couple of days anyway," Vic said. "You may make another run over later this week, I don't know. But the aircraft will be tied up here tomorrow and the next day."

"Will we be flying?" Leo asked.

"No, we're going to be checking out Cubans on the 54s."

"I didn't even know we had any Cuban 54 pilots," Leo said. "What are they going to do?"

"As a matter of fact, we've got several Cuban C-54 crews. They've been over here in camp while you've been airlifting."

"How about you guys giving with some poop," I said. "All the troops are on the boats. The 26s are all armed — or most of them. Kickoff time must be getting pretty close."

"Well, closer than it was yesterday," Riley grinned.

"Oh, crap," Leo said.

"Stay in the sack as long as you feel like it in the morning," Vic said. "Hang loose. We'll be getting you some word pretty soon."

"Hang loose, my ass," Leo said. "That's all we ever hear. Hang loose. Stand by. We'll be in touch. Nobody ever knows their butt from a hot rock."

"If a scorpion ever bites Leo, he's a dead scorpion," Connie said.

Wednesday morning, April 12, got off to a steaming hot start. An aircraft running up on the end of the runway woke me about nine o'clock. I was lying in a pool of sweat. Even though the tent's side panels were rolled up, there was no air stirring. The mosquito netting tucked in around my cot made it even more oppressive.

I pushed the netting aside and sat up on the edge of my cot. Leo was in the cot beside me. Both hands were under his head and his eyes were wide open. Without turning his head he said, "How in hell can you sleep with all that uproar?"

"What's the uproar?"

"The Cubans have been grinding around in the traffic pattern since seven o'clock this morning."

A C-54 at the end of the runway less than a hundred yards from our tent took off with a roar.

"How many of them are there?"

"Three," Leo said. "I wonder what the deal is. Looks like they're going to use the Cubans instead of us. Also I think they've already been briefed. Have you noticed how they all stay strictly in their end of camp?"

"I haven't noticed anything. I just opened my eyes."

"I'm not talking about right now. I'm talking about the last couple of times we've been in and out of here. All the Cubans have been in their tents. They've been eating by themselves. They haven't been wandering around camp, and they haven't been hanging around the API (our beer-drinking tent named after the Airport Inn, a beer and barbecue joint back in Birmingham). Now they're being marched in formation to the crapper. I just saw Hal escorting six of them up the hill."

The six-hole privy was located on a knoll about 50 yards east of our tent. From the direction of the knoll came a fusilade of sharp rapping sounds, like two boards being slapped together. Framed screens on hinges were used as lids to cover each position in the facility. However, scorpions had been known to take up positions on the underneath side of the boards alongside the utility holes. One victim, ambushed on a late evening call, had been flown back to Miami lying on his stomach. Afterwards it became standard practice to give a few sharp raps with the screened lid before assuming final position. The whole thing was extremely inhibiting, and most of us suffered from some degree of irregularity throughout our stay in camp. It was a long time after I returned home before I could break myself of banging away with the toilet lid in the family bathroom.

In a few minutes a file of men appeared on the path leading from the knoll. They disappeared in the direction of the Cuban end of camp, with Hal McGee bringing up the rear.

"What do you think all this means, Leo? Have you gotten any scoop from anybody?"

"No, and neither have any of the other guys who've been over here awhile. Nobody's said anything about them flying. It looks like the Cubans are going to fly the B-26s, too. Did you know Joe and Ron left for Miami this morning?"

"Miami? What are they going to do in Miami?"

"Hell, I don't know."

"Let's go over next door and see if they know anything."

The B-26 pilots, who had been in camp for several weeks, lived in the tent next to the one that I occupied with Leo, Ernie, Phil, Gordon and Sandy. Other members of our crews were scattered in tents wherever they had been able to find empty cots. Don Gordon, Bill Peterson, and Al Walters were in the next tent when we ducked in under the side panel.

"Well look what the cat dragged in," Al said. "Have a beer."

"Beer? Hell, I haven't eaten breakfast yet."

'That's what I mean. Have a beer."

"Look, do you guys know anything?"

"We thought *you* would know something. You're the ones that have been doing all the flying back and forth."

"Do you mean to tell me you guys have been sitting here on your asses for three weeks and don't even know what's going on?" Leo said.

"We can't even get the time of day," Don said. "So we just relax and enjoy life on the Caribbean."

"We heard Joe and Ron left for Miami this morning."

"That's right. Riley sent for them about an hour ago. They came back and grabbed some shaving gear and said they were going to Miami on a C-46. And *they* don't know what they're doing."

"God amighty."

"You said it, Buck. How about pitching some horseshoes?"

"*Horseshoes?*"

"Horseshoes. Right out back of your tent."

"Let me have one of those beers first."

"See? Now you're beginning to get the idea. How about you, Leo?"

"Jesus Christ," Leo said.

We relaxed, pitched horseshoes, drank beer, raided other tents for books and magazines of any vintage, and speculated endlessly. Activity in the compound continued almost around the clock. Company brass were almost incommunicado. The highly restricted Cuban air crews continued to be shepherded around camp in small groups.

All personnel were restricted to the base, which meant that no one could drive the half-mile into Puerto Cabezas. Hard liquor became scarce, but the beer supply at the API seemed inexhaustible. Rumors piled on top of rumors. No one had any solid information, but the invasion forces *were* on their transports in the harbor, belts of 50-calibre ammo were being loaded and rockets installed under the wings of more B-26s. The time for the launching of the invasion of Cuba was obviously only a matter of hours away. Thursday morning, April 13, a Lockheed Super-Constellation, with U.S. Air Force markings plainly visible through a hastily applied coat of paint, landed on the runway at Puerto Cabezas. Julio Rebull, who was on ramp duty at the ammo shed, saw some of the passengers changing out of uniforms into civilian slacks and shirts before disembarking.

The dozen or so passengers were picked up by jeeps and driven directly to camp where they went into a five-hour huddle with our base commanders in the API. Tarpaulin side panels were lowered around all four sides and two company security officers stood guard to keep the parade of curious men scuffling up and down the company street out of earshot. The pilots remained on board the "Connie." With an auxiliary power unit running the air conditioner, they were in a lot better shape than their passengers who were parboiling in a closed up canvas tent for five or six hours. When the meeting broke up in the middle of the afternoon, the visitors were escorted on a brief inspection trip of our aircraft up on the line. Then they reboarded the Connie and took off before dark.

Leo, still as uninhibited as he was the day he signed on, encountered Vic at the compound gate. He asked Vic who the people were and what they were doing in camp. Caught off guard, Vic said that they were men who had come down from Washington to make a final audit of the company's accounts. When Leo reported this to us, we cracked up at the idea of a planeload of bookkeepers flying all the way from Washington to audit a set of books on the edge of an equatorial jungle.

As usual, Leo cursed the whole setup furiously. Leo never adjusted to security in any shape or form. He took it as a personal affront that we were not made privy to the complete plans for the campaign, and all of its operational details.

Naturally, we suspected that major decisions had been made at the meeting on Thursday. We had no way to even guess at what they might have been. There was no doubt in our minds, however, that whoever our visitors may have been, they could not have been less than highly impressed by the sight of our B-26s armed and ready to go. We had no clue, of course, that in the highest echelons of the administration back in Washington, purely military considerations no longer had a number one priority.

After the departure of the delegation of "bookkeepers," tension in the compound seemed to increase. Midnight oil was burned even later, and company brass became even more inaccessible to us peasants (Leo pronounced it "us piss-ants"). The nearest we got to anything from the horse's mouth was Don's report that Riley had said to him, "We're really getting close now."

On Friday, April 14, Riley came to our tent around mid-afternoon. He said that the troop transports would pull out that night, and that the first mission was scheduled for the next morning. For the first time we learned that Cuban pilots, exclusively, would fly the first mission. This created a storm of protest from our B-26 pilots. Riley tried to explain that the Cubans were so confident of success that they insisted on doing all their own fighting. Leo was ready for that one. "That's a lot of crap."

Riley said that the first strikes would be against Castro's air bases. He said that we knew where every single one of Castro's aircraft were tied down or hangared. In this quasi-briefing by Riley, there was not the slightest hint or suggestion that everything we had available would not be used. What we had available was 23 serviceable B-26s.

Riley also said that a strike on Sunday morning would concentrate on armored equipment, plus power plants, communications centers, and on anything left undone by the Saturday attack on the air bases. Riley did not indicate where or when the troops would go ashore, but it was a simple enough matter to extrapolate the progress of ships doing about ten knots, and figure out that the landing would occur sometime on Monday. It never occurred to anyone that the landing would be attempted in the dark, or that resistance would not have been softened by preliminary attacks by air on the beachhead area, or that the invading forces would go ashore without aircover by our B-26s—all of which is nothing more than standard operating procedure.

Our main concern at the moment was with our own role in the invasion. Although we have been described as "instructors" and "advisers," the fact is, our briefing at the time we were employed made it clear that we were being hired to perform combat missions.

We didn't buy the business of the Cubans being so confident of success that they insisted on doing the whole job themselves. With Leo, we thought that was "a lot of crap."

I wandered up to the line late Friday afternoon. The activity there was feverish. Long trains of 500-pound bombs were being pulled around on dollies and loaded into the bomb bays of the B-26s. Rockets hung under the wings of all the B-26s. Three C-54s were lined up across the field next to the ammo shed. A row of C-54s and C-46s was parked in the grass off the runway at the far end of the field.

Some of these aircraft had been flown in by the so-called "contract" pilots, all of whom were still in camp. Like the Cubans, these crews had also been segregated and they were more or less "confined to quarters" in one tent. They griped continuously about not being allowed to return to Miami. Mostly they beefed to each other in their own language, whatever that was. They would have no role in the invasion itself, but they would not be allowed to leave camp until the invasion was underway, or over.

I hadn't been asleep more than a couple of hours Friday night when the R-2800s began to crank up on the line. Within five minutes everyone in camp was awake and struggling into pants and boots. In the darkness at the end of the runway, 150 men gathered to watch the takeoff of the first strike against Cuba.

As each pilot got his engines running he pulled out and fell into the line of aircraft taxiing toward the takeoff position. The heavily loaded aircraft accelerated slowly down the runway. Red exhaust flames turned to bright blue as full power was applied. They were far down the runway when they broke ground. Wing lights were switched off. We watched each aircraft until the twin pinpricks of exhaust flames blended into the curtain of stars across the sky.

Bill Peterson was standing beside me in the dark. "I counted nine," he said.

"I counted nine," I said.

"Maybe this flight is for one target," Bill said. "The rest will be taking off later."

"What time is it?"

Bill looked at his watch. "Three-thirty."

A pair of headlights approached down the runway from the direction of the portable control tower in the center of the field. It slowed and turned off into the company street, easing through the crowd of men who were breaking up and wandering off toward their tents. Vic, Connie, Reid and Larry were in the jeep. It parked in front of the compound gate. Bill said, "Let's go down and see what we can find out."

Riley was in front of us, headed for the compound. "Hey, Riley," Bill called. Riley stopped and turned back toward us.

"Is that all, Riley?" I asked.

Riley didn't answer. He just looked at us, then hunched his shoulders and spread both hands wide. Riley was not happy.

Nobody went back to bed. Lights were on all over camp and every tent had its group of men huddled together on the edges of their cots. The cooks started early and the mess tent was filled before daylight.

Word spread swiftly when the B-26s were due to start arriving back at the field. We pilots already had the arrival time pretty well figured out. We knew the range of the B-26s, how much time it would take to fly from Puerto Cabezas to Cuba and back, and how much loiter time was possible. At nine o'clock a crowd began to gather again at the end of the runway.

"Here they come," someone said.

All eyes sought the distant speck in the sky to the east. In a few minutes we could hear the distant throb of engines. The first B-26 pitched out over the end of the runway less than 50 yards from where we stood. There was no apparent battle damage. The next aircraft carried the scars of the morning's work, however. There were several visible holes in the fuselage and a gaping tear in the right wing panel.

Three more aircraft landed within the next 40 minutes. All had some damage. Two still carried a rocket or two that had failed to fire. Four of the nine aircraft that had taken off failed to return.

The returning aircraft were guided to parking places. The crews were picked up in jeeps and whisked away to the compound for debriefing. No one got a chance to talk to the pilots.

Before Saturday morning's air raid, Castro's air force consisted of 18 planes—six Lockheed T-33 jet fighters; six ex-RAF Sea Fury prop-driven fighters, and six B-26s. Add to this a couple of C-47s and Raúl Castro's personal Aero Commander. The exact location of all these aircraft was known prior to launching the first strike. Saturday's mission was designed to destroy Castro's air force on the ground in an initial surprise attack. In April 1961, Castro well knew that an attack was coming, but he didn't know when. Therefore, had we launched all of the aircraft we had available, this first mission's objective was entirely feasible.

In April 1961, most of Castro's experienced pilots were in Czechoslovakia undergoing training on the MIG 21s that had been made available to the Cuban government. None of these jet fighters had arrived in Cuba and Castro's air capability was quite small.

Of the nine B-26s that took off on Saturday morning, one flown by Captain Zúñiga, flew directly to Miami. A few minutes out of Miami, Zúñiga shut down one engine and feathered the prop. The aircraft carried evidence of battle damage which had been inflicted on the ground at Puerto Cabezas before his departure.

Captain Zúñiga's flight was intended to establish that the attacks on Castro's air bases that morning had been conducted by defecting pilots from his own air force. Zúñiga was supposed to be one of these. This scenario was obviously designed for the eyes of the rest of the world. There was certainly no possibility that Castro would be under any misapprehension about what was taking place. Nor was there any possibility that the story would hold up long even under the most cursory examination.

The other eight aircraft that took off on Saturday morning were directed to three targets. Three of the aircraft attacked the airfield at Camp Columbia in Havana. Three attacked the air base at San Antonio de los Baños outside Havana, and two attacked the air base at Santiago on the southeast coast.

One aircraft was shot down and crashed in the harbor at Havana; one lost an engine to ground fire, flew to the Naval Air Station at Key West where the engine was repaired and the aircraft returned to service in Puerto Cabezas. Another B-26, running low on fuel, was forced to land at Grand Cayman Island, a British possession. After some delicate negotiations between governments, the aircraft was refueled, released and returned to base at Puerto Cabezas.

Confirmation of the results of the Saturday raid came quickly through intelligence reports and from air reconnaissance photographs. Considering that the number of aircraft launched had been severely limited, the mission was almost, not quite, successful. The element of surprise was complete. Our pilots had pressed home their attacks with great courage and determination. Twelve of Castro's 18 aircraft had been destroyed. He was left with two T-33 jets, two prop-driven Sea Furies, and two B-26s.

No one in camp explained why only eight B-26s had been launched to accomplish the vitally important purpose of this first raid. As many as 22 aircraft could have been launched, with the probable result that Castro would have been left powerless in the air for the rest of the campaign. If this had been accomplished the Bay of Pigs story would have had a different ending.

A heavy concentration of armored equipment, tanks, trucks and tractor-driven artillery in a field next to the Cuban military academy had been revealed by U-2 reconnaissance photographs. We were told that this was to be the target of a raid on Sunday morning. We learned late Saturday night that there would be no mission flown on Sunday. There was growing evidence of consternation in the higher echelons of command at Puerto Cabezas. The brass was sticking close to the operations shack in the compound, and they weren't talking. Larry, Al, Frank, Riley and Hal only left the wire enclosure to eat. Their demeanor was serious, discouraged, and did not invite intrusion.

We spent Sunday in idleness. There were a few desultory horseshoe contests back of the tent, but mostly we spent the day discussing the situation and speculating on the coastal area where the brigade would land the next morning. None of us knew enough about the southern coast of Cuba and its terrain to come up with an even halfway educated guess as to where that would be. We did know that whatever advantages had been achieved by the unexpectedness of Saturday's surprise attack were being rapidly dissipated by the failure to follow up.

We also believed that the delegation from Washington on Thursday was somehow responsible for cutting down to eight the number of aircraft that had participated in the Saturday strikes, although we were unable to arrive at a logical explanation. That something was seriously wrong became more evident as the atmosphere of foreboding increased in the compound.

There was considerable activity on the line all day Sunday. Battle damage was repaired; preflight inspections were made; aircraft was fueled and rearmed; bombs were loaded and rockets attached in preparation for the Monday mission. We logically assumed that this would be an all-out effort to provide cover for the troops going ashore, to finish the job on Castro's air bases, and to destroy power stations and communications facilities. It did not occur to any of us — not in our wildest imagination — that an all out attack with everything we had would not be flown on Monday.

Monday morning brought another surprise. Far from what we had expected, air activity was limited to intermittent patrols over the beach by one and two aircraft at a time. These aircraft flew up to the beach and back at intervals throughout the morning. There were no follow up attacks on Castro's air bases and his few remaining aircraft. Castro's air forces had had since early Saturday morning to put damaged aircraft back into service. They were uninterrupted in this task by any opposition from us.

Six hundred miles across the Caribbean, elements of the Cuban brigade were struggling ashore at the Bay of Pigs under virtually unchallenged attack by Castro's handful of operational aircraft. Castro's militia and armored columns had begun to move down the roads from the north and the east.

The story of the three-day battle at the Bay of Pigs has been told many times. Because I have no personal knowledge of what happened on the beaches and on the roads leading into the Zapata swamps, I can provide here only a brief summary drawn from accounts of Cubans who *were* there, some of whom I have talked with since.

The men of Brigade 2506 of the Cuban freedom fighters fought a courageous battle against overwhelming odds. They fought until there was nothing left to fight with. The plan which President Kennedy had cancelled as being "too spectacular," for which he had substituted a "quiet landing, preferably at night," and the cancellation of the Monday mission, had left Castro in command of the air over the beaches, and over the offshore waters of the bay.

If there was one turning point in the battle, it occurred early when Castro's planes sank the ships that carried arms, ammunition and communications equipment of the landing forces. They were left naked on the beach. They had truly been "dumped in Cuba."

The Bay of Pigs is a 20-mile indentation in the south coast of Cuba 75 miles southeast of Havana. It is entirely surrounded by dense swamps. Playa Larga is located at the farthermost reach of the Bay. The town of Girón is located on the south coast on the eastern side of the funnel-shaped entrance to the bay. San Blas is 20 miles north-northeast of Girón. Cienfuegos is 50 miles east of Girón on Cuba's southern coast. A major highway connects Playa Larga with Central Australia Province where a large sugar plantation and airport is located. Another highway parallels the east shore of the Bay of Pigs connecting Playa Larga with Girón. Girón is connected with Cienfuegos by a highway which parallels the southern coast of Cuba, and with San Blas where at a Y-intersection it continues northeast to Yaguarmas, and north-northeast to Covadonga.

Except for two narrow-gauge railroads, these highways provide the only access to Girón and the Bay of Pigs. By the same token, they are the only ways out. It was on these roads and in the air above that the battle at the Bay of Pigs took place.

The brigade forces started ashore before daylight on Monday morning, April 17. The brigade and its supplies had been transported from Puerto Cabezas on board six ships. They were the *Houston*, the *Río Escondido*, the *Atlántico*, the *Barbara J*, the *Caribe*, and the *Blagar*. The *Houston* and the *Río Escondido*, with all supplies on board, were sunk by Castro's air force planes soon after daylight.

The captain of the *Houston* managed to maneuver to within 250 yards of the west shore of the Bay of Pigs where he grounded his ship. Members of the brigade's Fifth Battalion went over the side into the sea. Some made their way to shore. Some were killed by strafing aircraft, others by sharks.

The *Río Escondido* went down at sea off Girón. Many of the troops on board were drowned attempting to swim ashore, or killed by aircraft fire and sharks. The other four ships departed the area after disembarking their troops into small, aluminum outboard motor boats. The American officers of all four of these ships had to contend with near mutiny by their crews.

One, the *Caribe*, steamed south and never returned to the scene. Eventually, the *Atlántico*, the *Barbara J*, and the *Blagar* rendezvoused 50 miles at sea south of Girón. The ships' officers were unable to persuade their crews to unload the cargo into LCUs for the trip to the beach. In the end, they unloaded the cargo themselves, but it never reached shore.

Brigade parachute troops under the command of Captain Alejandro del Valle dropped north of Playa Larga to hold the road from Central Australia Province. Their heavy equipment was dropped first and lost in the swamps. One unit was also lost in the swamps. Still another unit widely missed its drop zone. The road from Central Australia was left open.

One battalion of the Cuban freedom fighters under the command of Ernesto Oliva occupied the town of Playa Larga. This battalion held against overwhelmingly superior forces until the last round of ammunition had been fired. All resupply of ammunition was at the bottom of the Bay of Pigs. Armed with tanks, 75 and 57 millimeter recoilless rifles, mortars, bazookas, and automatic weapons for each soldier, Oliva's forces fought a battle that is a lasting testimonial to his leadership and to the training and determination of the men in his command.

On the eastern front an equally courageous and determined battle was waged at Covadonga, and on the road south of Yaguaramas and later at San Blas. In the end, superior numbers, the virtually unchallenged freedom of the skies enjoyed by Castro, and the final exhaustion of the brigade's ammunition prevailed.

By Wednesday afternoon the line of defense had shrunk to a perimeter less than three miles in diameter around Girón. The battle was ended. The invasion had failed. The operation was reduced to individual efforts to escape into the depths of the surrounding swamps, and in pitifully inadequate open boats out to sea. Much too late, President Kennedy, who exercised almost complete, personal operational control over the mission, authorized two U.S. Navy destroyers to escort the *Blagar*, the *Barbara J*, and the *Atlántico* to the beach to evacuate the remnants of Brigade 2506. "Hold on," they messaged the beach, "we're coming."

"How long?" asked Brigade Commander San Román.

"Three to four hours."

"That's too long. You won't be in time. Farewell, my friends, I'm sign-ing off."

At the air base in Puerto Cabezas we knew things were going from bad to worse. When they made their infrequent appearances outside the com-pound company personnel wore looks of deep concern. Only the people in-side the compound who had access to radio and teletype facilities knew what was happening.

In our tents by the end of the runway, all we could be sure of was that more than 48 hours had passed since the first mission was launched on Saturday. We knew that any element of initial surprise had been ir-retrievably lost. We learned through the grapevine that the Saturday raid had been partially successful, but we also knew that with only eight aircraft committed, the effort had been spread very thin.

At noon on Monday word filtered down that the landing had been made before daylight, and was still in progress. We learned that the landing had been made at a place called the Bay of Pigs. Without access to maps or charts, we couldn't determine where on the coast the bay was located.

On Tuesday six B-26s flown by Cuban crews took off from Puerto Cabezas before daylight. Once again the targets were Castro's air bases. Since the previous Saturday morning they had remained unmolested. When the aircraft arrived over their targets a heavy cloud cover obscured the ground. The aircraft did not carry enough fuel to hold until the cloud cover dissipated later in the morning. The mission was not a total loss, however. One of the pilots leaving the San Antonio de los Baños area turned southeast toward the Bay of Pigs. When he arrived over the beach, he found the clouds along the coast beginning to break. He found a hole, let down, and continued to fly contact, trying to orient himself and to iden-tify the limits of the enemy advance.

The B-26 was attacked by a Sea Fury. A B-26 is much slower than the single-engine Sea Fury, but it is also a very stable and maneuverable air-craft. In the hands of an experienced pilot it is possible to execute a turn with a much smaller radius than any conventional fighter can follow. If the fighter attempts to keep the B-26 in its sights, the pilot will be forced to tighten up the turn to a point where his aircraft will stall and spin out of the turn. If this happens at a low altitude, there will be no room for recovery.

Under attack by the Castro Sea Fury, the brigade pilot executed exactly those evasive tactics. The Sea Fury pilot, instead of breaking off the attack, attempted to turn with the B-26, stalled out of the turn and spun into the Bay of Pigs. A B-26 had brought down, if not shot down, one of Castro's fighters.

In a dog fight with another of Castro's fighters, one of the brigade

B-26s was badly damaged and forced to make a crash landing on the field at Girón. The pilot was injured, and the copilot killed. The C-46 that landed at Girón on Wednesday morning (with Ferd on board as navigator) picked up the injured pilot and returned him to Puerto Cabezas.

Another of the pilots on the Tuesday mission failed to return. Since the only air action took place over the Bay of Pigs, it was assumed that the missing aircraft had run out of fuel on the return flight to Puerto Cabezas and had ditched at sea, or had become lost and was down somewhere on land. A rescue search was launched from Puerto Cabezas but the missing aircraft and crew were never found.

Shortly after noon on Tuesday we learned that Vic and Connie were going up to the beach in B-26s. They took off together shortly after three o'clock. I have no idea how their flight was cleared with Washington. I doubt very much if it was.

Vic and Connie came in off the Bay of Pigs at Playa Larga on the deck. On the road north of Playa Larga where Oliva was holding, they discovered a convoy of 60 or 70 trucks heading towards Oliva's position. The trucks carried a force of almost 1,000 men. The two aircraft separated. Vic got the lead truck in the convoy with one rocket. Connie plugged the road at the other end by destroying the last vehicle in the line. The convoy came to a halt. Vic and Connie made pass after pass up and down the road, bombing and strafing the stalled trucks. They killed several hundred men and left the highway in flames over a stretch of two miles.

How Vic and Connie got away with the stuff they did is a mystery. The attitude in Washington, dedicated entirely to concealing United States participation in the attempt to overthrow Fidel Castro, would preclude any possibility that Vic and Connie would be permitted to engage in actions that could expose them to capture, or even to being identified if they were killed in action. My own guess is that no one in Washington knew what they were doing until after the fact. Not only did they go up to the beach by themselves on Tuesday afternoon, but when they got back they tried to organize a plan with me to load 50-gallon drums of napalm on a C-54 to be pushed out on top of Castro militia and equipment. The only thing that stopped us was that we couldn't figure out a way to get the drums out of the aircraft in flight.

Vic and Connie were a couple of real cowboys. Back in November they had been made available to President Ydigoras to assist in suppressing a revolt by elements of the Guatemalan officers corps. A group of officers under arrest at Fort Matamoros in Guatemala City had killed a colonel and a captain on the staff, and then made good their escape. They holed up in the military barracks at Puerto Barrios on the gulf coast, and from there tried to organize a rebellion against the government.

Vic and Connie, flying B-26s, attacked the barracks, bombed the airfield, and destroyed a radio station captured by the rebelling officers. The revolt was put down before dark on the day it started. Since President Eisenhower was still in office in November 1960, it can probably be assumed that this particular mission was approved in Washington.

As with all company personnel, it was impossible to penetrate beyond the anonymity that shielded Vic and Connie. With them it was strictly a case of "what you see is *all* you get." What you saw in Vic was a man who looked like a prize-fighter, a light heavyweight. He weighed about 175 pounds, had black hair and a tough-looking face that showed all the bone structure. There was no fat on his body. He looked as if he stayed in "shape" all the time.

Vic *looked* mean — a first impression that was immediately dissipated as soon as you talked to him. He was pleasant and friendly, quick to smile, and easy to engage in conversation. He did not particularly like to talk about airplanes and flying, perhaps because such conversations ran the risk of compromising his cover. What Vic liked to talk about was antique furniture and international law, both of which were hobbies of his.

One night Vic caught a ride with me from Puerto Cabezas back to Retalhuleu. It was a smooth, quiet night with nothing to do but let the automatic pilot fly the airplane. I started a conversation about the trains loaded with passengers that passed close to the base two times a day, and how those passengers could see all the C-54s, B-26s and C-46s lined up on the ramp, and everything else that was going on. I suggested that, by now, half the people in Guatemala must have a pretty good idea of what we were up to. Vic didn't have any problem with that. He said everyone in the world knew what was going on, but that there were only two ways to handle the problem with Cuba. We could go in openly with a couple of divisions of Marines, or we could run a covert operation like the one we were presently engaged in. Vic said that a covert operation was the only practical choice.

When it was all over, and a new government was installed in Cuba, we would deny that we had anything to do with it. No one would believe this. No one was expected to believe it. But it would be accepted. In other words, according to Vic, if we openly attacked Cuba with our own forces, and if, say, the Soviet Union had a mutual defense treaty with Cuba, then we would be forcing the Soviets to respond in accordance with the terms of that agreement. The Soviets don't want to be forced into an armed conflict with the United States any more than we want to force them. In a covert operation where we organize, supply and train a force of Cuban exiles, the Soviet Union may know exactly what we are doing, but as long as we continue to deny it, we avoid forcing the Soviets' hand. This was a rationale for covert operations I had not heard before, or since. It seems to make a certain amount of sense.

Connie was subordinate to Vic. They seemed to operate as a permanent pair. Together they had come to the Bay of Pigs operation from somewhere in Southeast Asia; just where in Southeast Asia, or what they were doing there, I could never even get a clue.

It was certain that both Vic and Connie had served in some branch of the military service. Unlike people like Al and Reid, who were simply detached for the moment from their own branches of the military, Vic and Connie were permanent, full-time employees of the company.

Connie was completely unlike Vic. Like Jake and Hoyt back in Birmingham, they were not two peas in a pod, but they, too, came off the same bush. Connie was physically unimpressive, somewhat less than average height. He was not fat, not soft exactly, but without muscles that showed. He had thin, receding brown hair and the unlined face of a teenager. Connie encouraged no familiarity. He spoke only when it was necessary and he limited his conversation strictly to the business at hand, and to as few words as possible. What went with all this, however, was a projection of unquestioned authority. Like everyone else who knows his job, and does it well, Connie did his with undeniable self-assurance.

Very soon after the arrival of the C-54 crews in Retalhuleu, Connie scheduled all of us for a "check ride," ignoring entirely the several weeks of recurrent training we had just finished in Ft. Lauderdale, and discounting completely the evidence of our capability that our mere presence on the job in Retalhuleu might suggest.

I had already completed two trips to the other side when I was called down to the line late one afternoon for my "check ride" with Connie. He was already in the right seat when I went forward into the cockpit.

"Let's go down to San José," he said.

I got the four engines running without assistance from him. It was not a smooth job. We were accustomed to a crew of three. Our flight engineer always handled the mag switches and the starters located on an overhead panel on the C-54. The pilots jockeyed around with throttles and mixture controls on the pedestal.

"You guys always fly with an engineer?" Connie asked.

"So far."

"Jesus Christ."

San José is a small city on the coast 30 miles from Retalhuleu. It is a resort-type town where people, mostly from Guatemala City, spend weekends and vacations on the beach. The airport has a paved runway 5,000 feet long, and no control tower. I circled the field in order to determine the runway in use.

Connie offered only minimal assistance. He adjusted the power settings I called for, and handled flaps and gear when requested. About a half-mile out on final Connie said, "Full stop."

When we came to a full stop on the runway, Connie said, "Let's take off the other way." I taxied on down to the end of the runway, turned around and ran through the takeoff checklist. At 70 miles per hour, Connie chopped the throttle on the number three engine. "Feather number three," I said, making no effort to abort the takeoff since there was enough runway left to reach takeoff speed on three engines. In practicing engine out procedures it is customary to simulate feathering the prop by setting up a zero thrust power setting on the failed engine. It was not considered an entirely safe procedure to actually shut the engine down and feather the prop. Connie actually feathered the number three engine while we were still in the takeoff roll. As soon as we were airborne, Connie chopped the throttle on number four.

"Feather number four," I called out — and he did.

We struggled around the traffic pattern on two engines, the other two being actually shut down and feathered. The airplane was light — no passengers or cargo, and not much fuel. At gross weight with two engines out I would have been halfway to Australia before I had enough altitude to start a turn back to the field. When we landed Connie said, "Okay, crank 'em up and let's go home." Back at the base, Connie was out of his seat and gone before I had everything shut down and secured.

Vic and Connie represent a comparatively new breed of warrior. They are few in number. They serve their country for the most part in remote areas of the world where the risk of getting killed is high, and where amenities that can make life reasonably bearable are often almost nonexistent. Day in and day out they risk their lives in roles and activities not even known to the people they serve. They have no prospect of reward — not fame, nor fortune nor glory. There are no handsome uniforms to identify them; no campaign ribbons or decorations to say where they have served and how well they have performed. They risk their lives, and they sometimes sacrifice their lives in complete anonymity. We may disagree, quite honestly and sincerely, with the transient policies of the government that issues their orders, but no one has reason to disown or be ashamed of Americans like Vic and Connie.

Tuesday afternoon Gil Hutchinson, a senior noncommissioned officer in the U.S. Air Force who was in charge of the communications center, came to me and said that Larry wanted me to get a crew together to make a drop from a C-54 at daylight. He said the aircraft was already loaded and ready to go.

I chose Phil Chapman to go with me. I would rather have flown with Gordon but I thought that there might be more supply missions to fly the next day, in which Gordon should be available as a first pilot. Ernie had a world of flying experience but I did not want to get into an argument with him over the beach about how to handle a drop. Fred Ealey was as much of an unknown quantity to me in Nicaragua as he had been in Ft. Lauderdale. I was still not convinced that Fred could handle the aircraft competently. I knew that if I got hurt, Phil could at least get us back. Sandy Sanders asked to go along as flight engineer, which was fine with me. Sandy may not have been the greatest with the books and manuals, but he was tough as a nail and a good man to have along if we should have to join the boys on the beach.

I planned to take along a couple of Tommy guns and station Sandy at the back door where he would not only push out the equipment bundles, but also blast away at any unfriendly aircraft that might get too close. He couldn't have hit anything, of course, but the muzzle blast of a gun firing from a supposedly unarmed transport might surprise an attacker long enough to make him miss on his first pass.

At seven o'clock Larry sent for the B-26 pilots. There were only three left in camp: Don Gordon, Bill Peterson and Pete Ray. Al Walters was in Grand Cayman to pick up the B-26 that had run short of fuel. Joe Hinkle and Ron Smith were in Miami standing by with two Lockheed jet fighters which they never used.

The pilots found Larry, Frank, Al, Riley and Hal in the operations shack. A montage of aerial photographs of the beach was fastened to one wall. Larry didn't waste time or words.

"Fellas, this thing is going to hell," he said. "A lot of the Cubans have quit and we need some volunteers for a mission in the morning." (I was told later that the Cubans' commander had come to Larry and said that due to the apparent hopelessness of the situation on the beach, he would not permit any more of his aircrews to fly, and had ordered them to stand down.)

Hal McGee and Riley Shamburger immediately volunteered. They were followed by Don, Bill and Pete. Larry turned down Hal and Riley on the grounds that they were operational people who could not be exposed to capture. Gonzales Herrera, one of the Cuban pilots, would not obey the order to stand down. He was not only willing but anxious to fly. The Wednesday morning mission, then, was limited to four aircraft. There was a general discussion of targets. Don and Herrera were assigned the roads running east of Girón to Cienfuegos, and northeast in the direction of Yaguaramas. Bill was instructed to take the road leading north out of San Blas toward Covadonga, and Pete was assigned to the western front and the road leading south out of Australia that Vic and Connie had hit on Tuesday.

After the briefing Riley and Don spent some time in the API. They discussed the next morning's mission. Riley sent Don to bed around eleven o'clock. Up to the time he took off the next morning, Don did not know, nor did the other pilots know, that Hal and Riley had been given last minute permission to fly.

I was in Doc Barr's tent when Riley found me at midnight. Riley informed me that the mission in the morning had been organized and that he wanted me to fly with him as an observer. (There were no dual controls in the B-26s. The only way a second pilot could do any flying was to swap seats with the pilot.) Riley said that he would get my C-54 mission handled, and that he would line up other C-54 pilots to fly as observers on the B-26s.

In my opinion, this was a sound idea. A trained and experienced pilot would know how to keep a sharp lookout for hostile aircraft while the pilot concentrated on his targets. I discussed the mission for a few minutes with Riley before he left to round up other C-54 pilots. I didn't know what assignments Riley made, or planned to make, but the deal didn't hold up for very long. As I passed the compound on the way to my tent, Larry stopped me and said that he had cancelled plans for the C-54 pilots to ride as observers on the B-26s. He said that he did not want to put his experienced pilots into B-26s as observers. I protested because I believed that the pilots would be effective. Larry was adamant. Wade Gray, the radio operator went with Riley; Leo Baker flew with Pete; Jack Vernon flew with Don, and Herrera already had his observer lined up. A Cuban flew with Bill and a flight engineer with the 117th Wing flew with Hal. Red Cornish was not assigned, and Sandy Sanders was already scheduled to fly on the C-54 drop mission with me in the morning.

When Riley and Don split up at the API earlier, Riley returned to operations where he and Hal were able to persuade Larry that the mission next morning offered the only hope of keeping the invasion alive, and that consequently every available aircraft and pilot should be committed to this last ditch effort. Riley won the argument and Larry was finally persuaded to permit Riley and Hal to fly the mission.

I had left word earlier for an orderly to awaken me, Phil and Sandy at three o'clock. The orderly woke up Phil who said that he would rouse me and Sandy. Phil bypassed me and woke up Ernie who agreed to get up and fly with him. Phil explained this later by saying that he thought I was still scheduled to go on the B-26 mission. I was sound asleep when they took off, and I slept right through the departure of the six B-26s. Phil and Ernie did not make it to the beach and returned to base with their load.

The B-26s were scheduled to take off in pairs at 30-minute intervals. Don and Herrera took off first at three o'clock, followed by Bill and Pete at three-thirty, and Riley and Hal at four. While they were taxiing to the runway, Herrera's observer leaped from the aircraft and disappeared into the woods. Herrera flew the mission alone.

After the first four aircraft departed, word came that the president had authorized U.S. Navy carrier-based jet fighters to fly cover over the beach for an hour between six-thirty and seven-thirty. Reid Doster says that he climbed up on Riley's wing and passed this information on to him just before he took off. None of the other pilots were informed that there would be Navy fighters flying cover over the beach.

Don used almost the entire length of the 5,000-foot runway to become airborne. The heavily loaded aircraft climbed slowly out over the dark water as Don concentrated intently on his instruments. He leveled off at 9,000 feet and established a cruise power setting that would give him 230 miles per hour. When he checked his guns high over the Caribbean they malfunctioned and would not fire. "I'll do what I can with the rockets," he said to Jack.

When he had been in the air a little more than two hours, Don began a rapid descent toward the sea. He flew the last 50 miles at 500 feet. Ahead of him Bill and Pete were chattering on the radio. Bill had found a concentration of militia and equipment on the road from San Blas to Girón. Pete did not say what targets he was attacking, but several times he expressed concern about his remaining fuel. He said that he might have to land somewhere before he could make it back to Puerto Cabezas. As Don approached the coast he heard Pete say, "We're going in." Don interpreted this as meaning that Pete was initiating an attack. These were Pete's last words. He probably meant that the aircraft had been hit and was not controllable. Pete and Leo crashed in an open field on a sugar plantation.

The coastline was obscured by low hanging, broken clouds as Don approached. Don turned west, trying to pick up the entrance to the Bay of Pigs. After a few minutes flying on a westerly heading, he realized that he had overshot his target and turned back. The cloud cover began to break as the sun rose higher.

After flying east for a few minutes, Don spotted Girón and the road leading toward Cienfuegos. The brigade forces had put out panels marking the limits of their lines. Beyond the panels Don found scattered rolling equipment and militia strung out down the highway for several miles.

His first pass was at a weapons carrier which he set ablaze with a rocket. Next he made a pass at a detail of militia in the process of breaking camp. He never could get his 50-calibre machine guns to fire. Reduced to nothing but the eight rockets he carried under the wings of the aircraft, Don made seven more passes along the highway, firing his rockets at scattered vehicles and personnel.

He took considerable ground fire in return. His eighth and last rocket did not fire. Although he was unaware of it, the rocket was hanging straight down under his right wing. Don saw nothing of Herrera and heard no transmissions from him.

Don made his last strafing run and turned south off the beach sometime after six o'clock. Five minutes later he heard Riley and Hal talking to each other. Don called Riley and told him that he had been unable to fire his guns, and that one of his rockets had malfunctioned. Riley and Hal

who were coming up on the coastline, elected to attack along the highway
to Cienfuegos, since Don had been able to do only a limited amount of
damage with his rockets.

"Did you run into any opposition, Don?" Riley asked.

"Nothing in the air. I think I got hit by ground fire in the right engine.
It's running rough and losing power."

"You going to make it back all right?"

"If it doesn't get any worse than this I'll be okay."

"How about our little friends," Riley asked. "See any of them?"

"Little friends?"

"We're supposed to have some little friends with us at the beach. You
know, the good guys."

"I didn't see anybody."

Riley was talking about the Navy jet cover that had been authorized.
Not having been informed, Don didn't know what Riley was talking about.
He found out a few minutes later.

Don heard Hal on the radio. "Okay, I'm going in. Where are you,
Riley?"

"I'm right behind you, on your right."

A minute later Riley said in a hoarse voice, "Hit, hit!"

Don thought Riley had gotten a hit on some target. Still flying south,
and well out to sea, Don keyed his own mike. "What did you get, Riley?"

Silence.

Again Don asked, "Hey, Riley. What did you hit?"

Silence.

Hal came on the air. "T-Birds! They got Riley."

Hal began repeating the Mayday call signal, asking for help from the
carrier. There was no reply. "Hey, Don. Can you get back here and give
me a hand?"

"I can come back, Hal, but I'm already about 20 miles out and I don't
have any ammo."

"Well, see if you can relay to the ship that we've got T-Birds back here."

Don caught a movement out of the corner of his eye. He looked out
to his left and saw an unmarked jet fighter pulling into formation on his
wing. Don said later that if he had not been strapped in, he would have
gone through the canopy when he saw the fighter. The jet's pilot tossed him
a casual salute. Don picked up his microphone and tried unsuccessfully to
make contact. Then he motioned with his hand, indicating that the pilot
should turn back to the beach. The jet's pilot quickly got the message and
peeled off in a 180-degree turn. Watching the jet turn back, Don saw two
more jets in formation higher and farther back. They also turned back to
the beach.

Trying to conserve fuel and to baby his rough engine, Don eased up to

5,000 feet, ducking in and out of widely scattered cumulus. He heard no more transmissions from Hal. South of Grand Cayman Island, which is 200 miles south of Giron, he heard Vic and Connie in radio conversation. They were on the way to the beach, but south of Don's position. Don relayed the message that Riley had been hit.

Vic came on the air. "Is he down?"

"I don't know."

"What's the situation up there?"

"I don't know. Hal and Riley came in after I left. I heard Riley say he'd been hit. Then Hal said that T-Birds got him. I couldn't see any firing from our side. I don't think they can hang on much longer. They're getting squeezed in from every direction."

"What about Hal?"

"I don't know. I was talking to him. Some of our little friends went back after him."

"Are they still there?"

"Far as I know."

"They'll be gone by the time we get there," Vic said. "We're pressing our luck, Connie. We'd better do a 180 and head back."

"I'm right behind you, Vic. I agree. I don't know what we could accomplish at this point, and we've already stretched our luck pretty far."

Don came back on the air. "Hey Vic. My last rocket didn't fire and I don't know what it's doing. I want to make a low pass when I get back to the field. Have somebody standing by in the tower when I get there to let me know what it looks like."

"Okay, we'll be standing by."

Hal was in the lead when he and Riley approached the coastline. The earlier cloud cover was breaking up rapidly. Hal led the two-plane formation down through a hole. Below the clouds, he caught sight of the runway at Giron immediately ahead. Hal banked steeply to his right, continuing his descent, and picked up the coastline highway.

Just beyond the bright colored panel set out alongside the road, the truck Don had set on fire was still pouring black smoke into the sky. Armored vehicles and troops were moving on the road east of the burning vehicle. It was here that Hal called asking Riley for his position. Riley was following Hal a quarter-mile behind and off his right wing. Hal opened up with his 50-calibre machine guns on a line of trucks. Finishing his pass, he pulled up and started a steep turn, getting in position for another pass down the road in the opposite direction. As he rolled out he saw Riley making a pass down the road. At the same instant he saw a stream of tracers hosing in from behind and to the right of Riley's plane. Two Lockheed T-33 jets were closing on him rapidly. For a split second, as Hal turned toward the three aircraft, Riley's plane, and then the two jets, were in his gunsight.

Riley's right engine exploded in flame. The aircraft heeled over sharply to the right. Riley made his last transmission that he had been hit, and Hal watched as the B-26, its right engine in flames, hit the water 200 yards offshore. The two T-33s flashed by Hal in a steep climb. Hal made a series of steep turns, trying to pick up the jets, but he never saw them again. Although Hal did not know about the Navy fighter cover, and never saw them, it is possible that the two T-Bird pilots did, and fled the area after shooting Riley down.

Don's right engine grew progressively rougher as he flew south toward Puerto Cabezas. The return flight to the base took three hours. Reid, Larry and Frank were in the control tower when he made a low pass down the length of the runway.

"That thing is pointing straight down, hanging by its tail," Larry told Don on the radio. "What have you tried?"

"Nothing yet, except all the switches and circuit breakers. I didn't know what the situation was."

"Go back out to sea, climb to altitude, and see if you can shake that thing loose," Larry instructed. "You can't land with that rocket hanging there. We've measured it and you've got about four inches clearance between the nose and the runway. If you land hard, or it shakes loose, you'll blow yourself and half the field to hell and gone."

Don climbed out over the water to 5,000 feet. For 30 minutes he tried everything in the book to shake the rocket loose. Nothing worked.

"I've tried everything," he radioed the base, "and nothing works. I'll have to come back in and land."

"Hold everything," Reid said. "I think you'd better come back across the field at about 4,000 and bail out. Head the aircraft back out to sea before you jump."

"Papa, I've put six G's on this flying machine. If that won't pull that thing loose, it's not going to fall off when I grease this baby in on the runway. Besides, I don't think my associate here in the right seat, with his head down on his knees, will get out of this airplane unless I throw him out."

Everyone else was in favor of having Don land rather than to attempt to bail out. A B-26 is not easy to get out of. The canopy, instead of sliding back, opens up like a clam shell, creating a considerable obstacle to getting out of the cockpit.

After a short conference on the ground, Larry radioed Don, "Just make sure you *do* grease it in. Remember, you've only got a few inches between the head of the rocket and the runway. Land well down the runway — *after* we get out of the control tower."

"Gee, thanks for the vote of confidence. Don't you all trample each other to death bailing out of that tower."

Jack Vernon, who was riding shotgun with Don, said he never felt the aircraft touch down. The wheels just started rolling on the runway. On the ground, they learned that Pete Ray and Leo Baker had also been shot down.

When I left my tent Wednesday morning I went directly up to the line. It was eight-thirty when I reached the control tower (mounted on the back end of a flatbed truck) at the center of the field. The control tower operator was listening to a Spanish language broadcast on a shortwave receiver. When I started to speak, he raised his hand to silence me. He was intent on the broadcast which was difficult to pick up behind the static. "It's from Havana," he said. "They got one of our planes."

"Who was it?"

"They say they've got the bodies of two American fliers. The only name is Leo Berle."

Berle was Leo's "phony." I felt a sudden chill. For the first time since we left Birmingham I felt the full impact of the fact that we were not playing games, that this was for real. I started to walk, fast, back to camp. A jeep was coming down the runway toward me. Larry and Al and another company man stopped beside me.

"Have you heard the broadcast from Havana?" I asked. "It sounds like they got Pete and Leo."

"Yes. Riley, too," Larry said. "You've flown 51s haven't you, Buck?"

"Yes, I have. Some time back. I don't have a lot of time on them."

"We've got some 51s [the North American P-51, Mustang, one of the best fighters in World War II] in from Managua. We've about got the Nicaraguan colors painted out, and we're hanging external tanks and rockets on them. Can you take five Cuban pilots and go up to the beach?"

"Operate from the beach?"

"Right," Al said. "We've got fuel. We can fly ammo in. One 46 landed up there this morning. Now, Buck, these boys are young. None of them have much time, but they've all flown some single-engine stuff. You'll have to tell them what to do."

"Are they ready? How much time do we have?"

"Another two or three hours and they ought to be ready. You should have two or three hours of good daylight left when you get to the beach. We'll send the boys on up. You can be talking to them."

"How about a dash-one (the aircraft operating manual)? It's been a few years since I've been in a Mustang."

"There's a Nic pilot over there," Al said, motioning to the far side of the field where six Mustangs had been parked. "He's going to work with you, and he's got a manual."

Al said to come by operations and look at some aerial photos. The jeep headed back toward camp. I walked across the runway toward the hard-stand where the long-nosed fighters were parked.

By comparison with the C-54s I'd been flying, they seemed tiny and stubby-winged. Fortunately for me, my flying career, in the military and out, had not chained me to one or two particular types of aircraft. At that time, I had flown more than 40 different types even including a couple of crop dusters. It's like riding a bicycle, it may take a couple of hours of practice before you can say "Look, Ma, no hands!" but you don't forget how.

It was nine-thirty and the sun was like something freshly tapped from an open hearth furnace. Sweat streamed from every pore—probably for more reasons than the heat of the day. Puerto Cabezas, Nicaragua, was a long way, and a long time, from Canada where I had last flown a Mustang 19 years earlier.

I found some of our own ordnance people working on the Mustangs. They were loading belts of 50-calibre ammo into the wing lockers, and installing rockets under the wings. A paint crew was working on the last of the six aircraft, painting out the Nicaraguan rondels on the wing tips, and the colors from vertical stabilizers.

A Nicaraguan Air Force pilot was squatting under a wing of one of the aircraft. "Well," I said, affecting a nonchalance I did not feel, "I guess we're going to borrow some of your airplanes for a while."

"Sí." The pilot remained in his squatting position.

"Have you got a book, a manual I can be looking at?"

Without answering, the Nicaraguan pilot stood up, walked around to the far side of the airplane, climbed up on the wing, and fished a thick manual out of the cockpit. "Here," he said.

Boy, I thought, this guy is going to be a big help. He acts as if I'm stealing his personal airplane. "You speak English, don't you?" I asked. "I've got some Cuban pilots on the way up here and I may need some help. I don't think any of them have flown a 51."

"Yeah, I speak English."

He not only spoke English, he spoke it very well. He had been trained as a military pilot by the U.S. Air Force—winding up for his advanced training at the Air Force base in Selma, Alabama.

He hated Alabama. He hated the United States, and he hated me. He was black. I mean, he was *African* black.

I remember thinking, only fleetingly, I'll admit, that to spend a quarter of a million dollars to train this guy to fly might be a good policy. To train a black, Spanish-speaking Nicaraguan in Selma, Alabama, in 1959, was like pouring that whole foreign policy investment in Nicaragua down a rat hole.

Since it didn't seem that the constricted dialogue between me and the Nicaraguan would develop productively, I climbed into the cockpit of the Mustang with the dash-one and began to reorient myself. It didn't take long for me to begin to feel at home. (Look, Ma, no hands.) The tarmac at

RCAF Station, Trenton, Ontario, no longer seemed so far away and long ago.

While I was exploring the cockpit, a jeep rolled up with five very young Cubans aboard. They dismounted and approached the aircraft with what seemed to me to be some reluctance — as if, maybe, someone might be following behind with a gun at their backs.

The first of several problems developed immediately. Only one of the Cubans could speak any English, and he was not very fluent. Through him, and with the help of the Nicaraguan pilot, I learned that none of them had much total time in the air. All but one had a few hours in the Sea Fury, a prop-driven fighter used by the British Royal Navy in World War II. The least experienced of the pilots had received advanced training on single-engine aircraft, but he had not flown high performance aircraft. This young pilot's entire operational training would consist of the flight between Puerto Cabezas and Cuba — providing he didn't ground loop on takeoff.

I could see that we were not going to be the greatest bunch of tigers that had ever taken to the air. In fact, I began to wonder if we would not be more of a threat to one another than a major threat to Castro.

I planned to give them all a thorough cockpit check and at least one circuit and landing before we all struck out for the beach. First, using the Cuban who spoke a little English, and the reluctant Nicaraguan pilot, I conducted a short course in air-to-ground support.

I described the tactics we would use over the target areas. We would fly in pairs. One aircraft would be the "gun." The second aircraft, "tail-end Charlie," would fly behind. His responsibility would be to protect the lead aircraft from attack by air, to spot sources of ground fire, and to locate targets of opportunity.

With half of his ammo remaining, the lead aircraft would swap places with number two who would expend all of his weapons load. Number two would land first to rearm and refuel, while number one, with half of his ammo remaining, flew cover over the field. Number one would land while number two flew cover.

Another problem was communications. We would be able to communicate between aircraft but not with the men on the beach. The radios in the Nicaraguan Mustangs did not have the right frequencies. Since I could not speak Spanish, and the Cubans could not speak English, some lack of coordination was inevitable.

I pointed all this out and explained that we would get a briefing on the situation on the beach before taking off, but once there, we would all have to select targets based on what we could find and interpret, and the intelligence available on the ground while refueling.

It was close to noon when we finished the briefing. I had done most of the talking, assisted by the Nicaraguan interpreter who began to show a little more interest when the discussion got around to tactics. However, there was none of the lively discussion you might expect from a group of pilots who were about to launch on an exciting and important mission.

The six aircraft were almost ready. One of the pilots mentioned lunch. I sent them ahead and told them to be back on the line in 40 minutes. An hour later they had not shown up. I started back toward camp to find my tigers. They were not in the mess tent. I walked up between the two rows of tents occupied by the Cubans. In one of the tents I found all five of my boys sacked out enjoying a siesta. I woke them up and said it was time to go to Cuba. They stumbled around muttering and grumbling in Spanish. I took a jeep that was parked in the street, stopped by the supply shack and drew six parachutes and a .45 automatic for myself, then drove up to the line. The ordnance men were gone and the Nicaraguan said that the aircraft were fueled and ready to go. I looked back across the field to see if my tigers were in sight. A jeep was racing up the runway. It was Al.

"Forget it, Buck, they've lost the field."

"No place to go, huh?"

"No place to go. Hop in and I'll give you a ride back. I've already intercepted your pilots."

I've wondered often if the traditional Spanish custom to enjoy a siesta after lunch didn't, maybe, save my life.

One final effort to salvage the situation at the Bay of Pigs was also aborted later Wednesday afternoon.

Larry sent for me about two o'clock. "Buck, there's a 54 loaded and ready to go. Ernie and Phil didn't make it in to the beach this morning and they brought their load back. They're out of everything up there. I want you to get a crew together and make a drop. The load is on rollers, so all you have to do is push the bundles out the door. You'll have to hurry. Get your guys together and get back here as quick as you can and we'll give you the picture."

I found Gordon in the tent. He agreed to fly with me. "Who can we get for flight engineer?" I asked.

"Red Cornish is down eating right now. Get him."

I found Red and a half-dozen other men having lunch. "Come on, Red. We've got to fly a drop mission right away."

Red didn't respond. He didn't look up from the table. Red didn't want to go. It was embarrassing and I didn't know what to do. After all, this is what we had come down here for. More than that, though, I realized what Red was doing to himself. What a hell of a thing — to have to spend the rest of your life knowing that you have come up short, that you had failed yourself. I didn't want Red to do this.

I tried again, trying to make a joke of it, trying to be funny. "Aw, come on, Red, you can finish that steak when we get back."

Red didn't move. "I can't go, Buck," he said in a barely audible voice.

There was an awful moment. Everyone else had stopped eating. Then Sandy Sanders broke the silence. He stood up and said, "You need a flight engineer? How about me going with you, Buck?"

I looked at Sandy. He was red-eyed. He had already flown six hours with Ernie and Phil before daylight that morning.

"Okay, Sandy, come on."

On the way back to the compound I told Sandy to go by supply and get parachutes for everyone, plus .45s and two Tommy guns.

"Are you going to be able to get those bundles out by yourself?" I asked Sandy.

"I looked the load over this morning," Sandy said. "It's all on rollers. I'll get everything out all right."

"Okay, me or Gordon will come back and give you a hand if you need any help."

"Don't you want me to get three Tommy guns, Buck, so we'll each have one?"

"Sandy, I'm not planning to land up there on the beach. Those are for you to shoot out the back door with."

"Hey. That's a good idea."

"I don't know if it is or not. You couldn't hit a bull in the ass with a bass fiddle, much less one of those Thompsons."

Gordon was in the operations shack with Larry, Al and Frank. Four Cubans were standing in one corner of the room. They had been asked to make the drop, but by now most of the Cubans considered themselves to have been grounded on orders of their own leaders.

Larry pointed to the recon photos on the wall. "I don't know how much good this will do," he said. "We don't know exactly how much ground they're still holding, but it's not much. Maybe some of this stuff will help some of them get off the beach. It's about all we can do for them now."

"How high should I be to make the drop?" I asked. "I guess it doesn't make much difference. If the bundles are going to bust open, they'll bust from 50 feet as easy as they will from 200 or 300."

"Three hundred feet ought to be plenty high enough," Al said. "If you want to go lower, okay. Just don't get up where you'll attract any attention. You shouldn't have any trouble except from ground fire."

"Don't worry," I said. "The props on your airplane are going to be all knicked up from sand and gravel when I get back here."

"Okay, and if you don't see any people on the beach anywhere, drop the stuff in the swamp. Maybe somebody will pick it up." Larry turned to Gordon and handed him a set of charts. "You got the frequencies?"

"Sí," Gordon said, showing off his Spanish.

One of the Cubans in the corner followed us out the door. "Hey," he said, "I'm going also if you'll let me. I can help push."

"You want to go with us?" Gordon asked.

"You fellows want me to go along also?"

"Come on, Senor," Gordon said, "also."

It was a few minutes after three when we pulled up in the jeep alongside the C-54. Sandy was already there, inside the aircraft. Our new Cuban friend went up the ladder and through the cargo door. Gordon was halfway up the ladder when I saw a jeep coming down the runway. The first thing I thought was that we had forgotten to pick up a chute for the Cuban — which we had — and that someone was bringing one to us. However, it was Frank.

"Okay fellas, climb down," Frank said.

"What now?"

"They're wiped out," Frank said. "You'd just be dropping this stuff to the bad guys."

"Well, in other words, that's the old ball game?"

"That's the ball game," Frank said. Then he added, "No hits. No runs. All errors."

Aftermath

Wednesday night at the API, Hal McGee told me of a proposal he had made to the command staff at Puerto Cabezas shortly after his return from the Wednesday morning mission. Hal's proposal was that we salvage the operation by creating an incident which would provide the United States government with a "legitimate" excuse to send in the Marines and naval forces.

Following the first attack on Saturday morning, Castro began trumpeting in rage and leveling charges of aggression at the United States. Suppose that Castro in his excitement and rage had been so ill-advised as to retaliate with an attack on our naval base at Guantanamo Bay, an act that some could have seen as predictable, even justified, and in any case, not at all beyond the limits of credibility.

Such an attack would demand an immediate response from the U.S. government with, say, a couple of divisions of Marines that just happened to be on maneuvers in the area at the moment. Clearly this response would have been an action in self-defense, not one of aggression. It would also have marked the end of Castro's reign, which was the worthy object of the whole exercise at the Bay of Pigs in the first place.

Hal's proposal was to fake the incident by flying two of our B-26s (which already carried Castro's Air Force markings) from Puerto Cabezas up to Guantánamo and stage a raid on the Navy base. The idea was to make a couple of strafing passes and drop a couple of bombs in a far corner of the airfield. The area would be cleared beforehand, and cameras would be ready to record the dastardly attack. For sheer cynicism, of course, it would be hard to match this plan. As a quick and certain solution to a serious problem, it would also be hard to match. Hal told me later that he had heard that his proposal went all the way to the White House where President Kennedy vetoed it. ("Muffed it" is the way Hal put it.)

On Thursday Al Walters brought the stranded B-26 in from Grand Cayman Island. A few hours later Joe Hinkle and Ron Smith arrived from Miami with a C-46. They had an interesting story to tell.

When they left Puerto Cabezas they were told they were going to

Miami, nothing more. They landed at Opa-locka before daylight and were confined to the base throughout the invasion. All they could learn about what was happening at the Bay of Pigs was what they read in the Miami newspapers and heard on the radio.

Although they practically got down on their knees, none of the company personnel at Opa-locka would tell them anything, least of all why the two of them had been flown to Miami just as the action was getting underway.

On Wednesday, after almost a week of inactivity and frustration, Joe and Ron were told they had been brought to Miami to test-fly a C-46 and take it back to Tide. Word had already spread through the news media that the invasion was floundering. The C-46 story sounded completely fishy.

"Look," Joe said, "if all we came up here for was to test-fly a C-46 and take it back to base, you could have told us that the day we got here. We could have been back down south by now. You know we're not going to buy that crap, so how about it fellas, what's happening down there, and what in hell are we doing up here?"

"Well, okay," a company representative said. "We've had two jets here all the time. That's what you're up here for. I should say that's what you *were* up here for, to fly two T-Birds if they needed you. They didn't use you, and don't ask me why. And now you really *are* going to fly a C-46 back to base, so you might as well get ready."

The final statistics after the air action at the Bay of Pigs reads something like the statistics after a football game where the team with the most first downs, the most yards rushing, and the most yards passing, lost the game. After the Saturday morning raid, Castro had only six serviceable aircraft he could put in the air. We on the other hand, even after the game was all over, still had 15 or so B-26s, six Mustang fighters, two jet fighters, and a ramp full of transports.

Now I know where the expression *c'est la guerre* came from. Things began to shut down rapidly at camp. Within 48 hours after the last shot was fired at the Bay of Pigs, a large delegation of Nicaraguan army officers appeared in camp. They spent the better part of an afternoon in conference with our headquarters staff. General Somoza, the president's brother, led the group. It seems that the Nicaraguan government was beginning to suffer from a severe case of nerves. The fact that the invasion of Cuba had been staged from Puerto Cabezas was no secret to anyone anymore, much less to Fidel Castro. A map, complete with "X" marks and arrows showing the exact location of Puerto Cabezas and the routes of flight to the southern coast of Cuba, appeared in the April 21st edition of *Time*.

The day after the visit of the Nicaraguans, we began flying patrols in B-26s from daylight to dark up and down the coast of Nicaragua. Our orders were to prevent any aircraft from penetrating the air space around

Puerto Cabezas. We were instructed to fire across the bows of any aircraft attempting to do so. If they kept on coming, we were supposed to confer with base by radio about shooting them down. The possibility of a Castro counterattack was very much on everyone's mind. An airborne assault by one well-equipped battalion, for instance, could have taken the base without trouble.

Don and I flew several of these day-long patrols together, munching on baloney sandwiches, which we washed down with warm Coke. Once we scared the daylights out of a C-54 crew bound for Miami when we sneaked into tight formation with the aircraft. We were glued in formation on its left wing for at least 30 minutes before the captain glanced casually out his side window and saw us sitting almost in the cockpit with him. He went into a violent spiral dive that must have covered the ceiling in the passenger cabin with cold beer and cubalibres.

Don allowed me to take out all my frustrations on a small, acre-sized, uninhabited island ten miles offshore. At the end of each patrol, I "attacked" the island on the way back to base. Palm trees and coconuts were blown to bits. If we had continued with the patrols for a week longer, I would have sunk that island.

The Nicaraguans were intent on getting us out of the country as soon as possible, along with all the evidence that we had ever been there. (This did not extend to the B-26s which the Nicaraguans "inherited.")

Flights left every day for Miami. Larry, Al, Frank, Vic and Connie left almost immediately. The so-called "contract" crews were gone. Gil Hutchinson was busy burning papers in the incinerator in the compound. Doc Barr drove out to a Catholic mission deep in the interior where he presented a sizeable supply of medical equipment to the nuns in charge. He also made a present of his entire supply of penicillin to a mission hospital in Puerto Cabezas. The hospital was overjoyed to get it although they wound up having to shoot most of it into some of our guys who organized their own foreign relations program which they pursued in town every night.

At four o'clock in the afternoon of the third day following the collapse of the invasion, I was called from my horseshoe game to see Burt, who was now the ranking company man in camp. Burt instructed me to get a crew together for a flight to Homestead Air Force Base in Florida with a plane load of "mutineers." I learned for the first time of the prison stockade that had been maintained deep in the Guatemalan interior.

The stockade had been set up many months earlier to hold the wide assortment of dissidents that always show up in the ranks of a military organization. This group included AWOL's, deserters, Castro agents who had infiltrated the ranks of Brigade 2506, common criminals (there was a murderer), and a handful of men who had apparently talked about organizing a revolt against company and brigade authority back in the winter months. I suppose that it was this latter group that inspired the use of the term "mutineers."

In all, there were 66 prisoners. They had been brought in and held for several days on a ship in the harbor at Puerto Cabezas. Burt's instructions were to fly them to Homestead just outside Miami. Burt reminded me that there were many among the prisoners who would much prefer to go to Havana than to Miami. He instructed me to have everyone in the crew draw weapons, and he said that I was to inform the prisoners before takeoff that anyone who so much as rattled the door between the cabin and the cockpit would be shot.

"Do I mean that?" I asked.

Burt said that I was not to hesitate to carry out this order, and that I could answer questions later at Homestead.

Gordon, Sandy, Ferd and I made up the crew. We all drew .45s and Sandy still had one of the Tommy guns he had drawn earlier for the flight up to the beach.

The C-54 was ready on the line when we drove up in our jeep. So were the prisoners who were still on the trucks that had brought them up from the ship. A company security man, another "Jim," was waiting for us with a set of scales. He had an idea that we would want to weigh the men when they went on board with their hand luggage. I explained that we were not worried about over-grossing the airplane, and that it would be unnecessary to weigh them. I also said that I did not want any of the "mutineers" to carry any baggage, bundles or packages on board the airplane. I wanted everything stowed in cargo holds that were inaccessible to the cabin in flight. I asked the security man, Jim, to have the men form in a single file and go one at a time to the cargo hold under the airplane where I stationed Sandy. After they disposed of any luggage they were carrying, they were to board the airplane and sit down. First, however, I wanted Jim and Gordon to shake each man down before he went up the ladder. Jim said all the men had been shaken down before they got off the boat.

"Well, let's shake them down again," I said. "One more time won't hurt anything."

We found a large cardboard box. The first "mutineer" gave up a tablespoon so sharply honed that a ten-year-old child could have disemboweled a gorilla with it. This was followed by an assortment of switchblade knives, a wrench or two, sharpened files, even a couple of handguns, minus ammo clips. When the last man climbed the ladder into the cabin, the carton was filled halfway to the top. Jim was somewhat dismayed. "Well," he said, "they must not have shaken them down too good."

"No, and there's no telling what's in those bundles and suitcases. They can't get at any of that stuff in flight, but I'll tell the people in Miami to go through it good."

I stationed Ferd inside the door where the men came on board the airplane. I went forward and stood in the door to the cockpit. The prisoners came up the ladder and into the cabin one at a time. Ferd instructed each man to find a seat. I looked each man over carefully as he came on board, hoping to find some sign that would tell me if, and where, trouble might be anticipated. They all looked like trouble to me. They all looked tough enough to eat a hole through the side of the airplane if they felt like it. Of course the months they had spent in the jungle stockade, and their more recent confinement on the ship at Puerto Cabezas, had done nothing to improve their appearances.

They were all sizes, shapes and colors. One man was well over six feet four inches tall. He looked to be half Chinese and half Negro. His head was hairless and he wore an oriental type of mustache that drooped at the ends. He looked like a villainous, giant-sized Yul Bryner. Overall, he was the most complete personification of evil I have ever seen.

The cabin filled quickly. Almost one third of the men had to sit on the floor. When they were all on board, Gordon went forward to the cockpit with Ferd. Sandy closed and locked the door at the rear, then he went forward to the cockpit, banging the Tommy gun around noisily. I asked for someone who could speak English. A man sitting at my feet spoke up.

"Okay. Stand up here and repeat exactly what I say. Make sure that everyone understands. First, tell the men that we are going to Miami. This will be a six-hour flight. They are permitted to smoke when we are in the air. Use the cans that are furnished for ash trays."

I nodded to the interpreter and he rattled off a rapid stream of Spanish. While he was talking, I watched the prisoners and quickly divided them into three categories. Some of them were gazing out the windows or staring at the floor. Others watched the interpreter as he spoke. A few never took their eyes off me. Among these last was Fu Manchu. I wondered if they were trying to make up their minds about anything.

"Now," I said, "tell them that I do not know who will meet them in Miami, where they will go or what plans have been made for them. Tell them that I know nothing other than that I have been instructed to fly them to Miami."

The interpreter rattled that off.

"The last thing is this. All of the men must stay where they are throughout the flight, except that they can go to the bathroom, one at a time, there at the rear of the cabin. No one is to come forward. If anyone opens, or attempts to open this door, he will be shot."

There was a longish pause, then the interpreter translated. I couldn't see any change of expression on anyone's face. The giant Chinese didn't blink an eye — and he didn't take his eyes off me.

"You're sure everyone understands? They got it okay?"

"Sí, they got it."

The flight to Miami was uneventful. We flew north out of Puerto Cabezas to a point just east of the Nicaraguan-Honduran border. Then we took up a northwest heading across Swan Island, checked our position abeam of Belize, used the Cozumel, Mexico, radio beacon to steer through the Yucatan Channel and past the west tip of Cuba, and turned north again to a dead-reckoned position in the Gulf of Mexico due west of Ft. Myers, Florida.

"Time to turn and start letting down, Buck," Gordon said.

"Okay. Down to 250 feet?"

"Right. And you'd better let it on down. We're supposed to be at 250 by the time we're 100 miles out of Ft. Myers."

"See if you can get Ft. Myers," I said.

"I've got it set up. We're still too far out. Okay, Buck, coming up on 900 . . . eight . . . seven . . . six . . . five . . . four . . . three, and 250. Hold her right there."

"I hope that radar altimeter's working. I can smell salt water."

"It's called sweat," Gordon said.

"Yeah — cold. I think I'm picking up some lights, or reflections."

"Yeah, Ft. Myers is coming in. Looks like left about ten degrees to zero-seven-five. Everything is all right back there, Sandy?" Gordon called over his shoulder.

"They're all asleep," Sandy said.

"How about you?"

"I'm asleep, too."

"Well, you'd better wake up. And park that cannon."

"I've got the shoreline," I said. "I think I'll swing right to miss the middle of town and the airport. Isn't that the field off there to the left?"

"Yeah, the airport's north of town. Good idea to swing south a little."

"My God, we're low," I said. "I think we must be picking up spray. The only radar that could pick us up would have to be on a submarine."

"Don't sneeze."

"Don't worry, I'm not even breathing."

The lights of Ft. Myers raced backward below the wings of the aircraft. It was after midnight. The streets were empty of traffic.

"I hope there aren't any TV antennas out here," I said.

"I've checked the chart. We're okay."

"What's the date on that chart — 1927?"

"I've got Homestead set up," Gordon said, pointing to the omni bearing indicator. "Swing over and pick up that two-five-five radial. We won't have anything but alligators underneath us all the way."

A glow from the lights of Miami was beginning to show on the horizon. "I think I see Collins Avenue and the Pussycat Club," I said.

Gordon picked up his mike. "Ah, Homestead, this is Lima One."

"Go ahead Lima One."

"Lima One is 15 DME west for landing."

"Roger, Lima One. Radar contact. What's your present altitude and point of departure?"

Gordon looked at me inquiringly. I just shrugged my shoulders and raised my eyebrows.

"Ah, Homestead," Gordon said, "we don't have that information."

There was a significant pause before another voice, more authoritative in tone, responded. "Lima One, enter downwind for runway three-five. Altimeter three-zero-one-zero. Wind light and variable. Stay with me after you land and follow the vehicle that will be out to guide you in. Come on up to traffic pattern altitude, and you can show some lights now."

"Okay, understand runway three-five," Gordon said. "Coming up downwind."

"In sight downwind, Lima One. Clear to land."

Before we had rolled to a stop on the runway a jeep raced forward under our wing and pulled up ahead of us. There was a "follow me" sign attached to the back of the jeep. Four Air Force security police armed with automatic weapons were inside. The jeep guided us to a remote corner of the field. I switched off the taxi lights, cut the engines, and opened the window beside me. Sandy went back and opened the door. I stuck my head out the window. The beams of a dozen flashlights were moving around on the ramp. I looked back along the length of the airplane. Two or three flashlights were climbing the ladder into the cabin. After a minute or two my eyes became accustomed to the darkness and I could make out forms moving around under the wing. I recognized Eric standing just below my cockpit window.

"Howdy, Eric."

"Is that you, Buck?"

"That's me."

"Well, I'm happy to see you. Have your crew stand by there in the cockpit for a few minutes until we can get your passengers checked out and off the aircraft."

Eric hadn't changed, except that he was in uniform. As Gordon put it, he was "dressed up in his Major's suit."

We stayed in the cockpit for 30 minutes while the prisoners were unloaded. On the ramp outside I saw a couple of familiar looking vans. The aircraft was ringed by security police carrying automatic weapons. When the last of the prisoners were off, we walked back through the cabin and climbed stiffly down the ladder to the ramp. We all shook hands with Eric.

The prisoners were loaded into the vans and driven away. I don't know what happened to them. They had not violated any U.S. or local

laws. Maybe they were just taken downtown and let out on the corner of
Flagler Street and Biscayne Boulevard. On the horizon, the lights of Miami
glowed against the sky. It had been a long time since we had seen the lights
of a big city.

"Hey, Eric, how about going into town for a couple of hours?" Gordon
asked.

"Gentlemen, I'm afraid you're as close to Miami as you're going to get
for a while," Eric said. "We have some coffee for you, and a gas truck is on
the way. You'll have to take off as soon as you've been refueled. We want
you clear of the coast and well out to sea before daylight."

"Eric, you're a doll," Gordon said.

Eric was right, though. We were indeed well out to sea at daylight. In
fact, it was only nine-thirty in the morning when we lowered the gear on
final at Puerto Cabezas.

There was no sign of life on the field when we landed, and no activity
in camp. We were reduced to a skeleton crew. Burt and a handful of company administrative personnel were in the compound. The Birmingham
people were still in camp, but they began to leave at the rate of one or two
a day until Bill Peterson, Joe Hinkle, Gordon, Ron and I were left.

The Cuban air crews were still in camp. Two nights later, Gordon and
I flew them to Homestead Air Force Base. Finally, the last of the C-54s was
flown out and we were left with only one C-46. Ten days after the invasion
the B-26 patrols were discontinued. The Nicaraguans were a lot more in
evidence and a lot less friendly. Armed Nicaraguan guards patrolled the
field and stood guard over the B-26s, all of which were turned over to their
Air Force.

The few of us remaining managed to engineer one final fiasco before
we pulled out of Puerto Cabezas. The military commander of the district
in which Puerto Cabezas is the principal city, was a Nicaraguan Army Captain named Cardonas. Captain Cardonas had his quarters with the small
Nicaraguan Air Force unit at the far end of the field. From time to time
throughout our stay at Puerto Cabezas, we were called on to perform small
favors and occasionally to provide transportation for Captain Cardonas
and other members of the Nicaraguan military establishment.

One morning shortly before our departure from Puerto Cabezas, Ron
flew Cardonas to Managua. He was scheduled to go back and pick him up
the next day. That night someone had the bright idea that we should all go
back to Managua right that minute, spend the night in the city, and pick
up Cardonas for the return trip in the morning.

Ron, Joe, Burt and I piled into the C-46 and took off. Ron, who had
been to Managua a couple of times before, swore that he knew all the
"ropes," and that we would have no difficulties. We all carried phony paper
and may well have encountered some "difficulties" if we had run into a

situation that required explaining our presence and exhibiting passports or tourist cards.

We landed at Managua at eleven-thirty and taxied to the military side of the field. Ron managed to convey to the personnel on duty that we had been requested by Captain Cardonas to come in that night so that we could make an early departure the next morning.

We found a taxi driver who spoke a little English, and we kept him with us while we checked into the hotel and then toured the night spots of the city. When everyone ran out of money in the small hours of the morning, we returned to the hotel. We instructed the cab driver, whom we had not paid, to meet us at the hotel in the morning to take us back to the airport.

Our plan was to locate Captain Cardonas and put the bite on him for the hotel bill and the taxi. This all sounded great at three-thirty in the morning. Things weren't quite so rosy when we met for a subdued breakfast at nine-thirty. Ron called the field and couldn't locate Captain Cardonas.

The language barrier prevented us from conveying all the nuances of our situation on the telephone. The cab driver, with whom we had run up a sizeable tab, spotted us in the lobby and was lurking in the entranceway to the hotel. Our biggest danger was that Captain Cardonas would go to the field and, in our absence, find another ride back to Puerto Cabezas — leaving us on the beach in Managua with our billfolds stuffed with bogus identification papers and no money.

Ron made a couple of trips to the desk to get the hotel operator to call the field for us. We were beginning to attract attention. The clerk at the desk kept looking at us suspiciously and turning to talk to the switchboard operator. We were beginning to have visions of languishing in a Nicaraguan jail for years. Then, Ron had another of his brilliant ideas.

All of us had been furnished with a list of telephone numbers to use in case of an emergency. There was a number for each country in Central America. However, the kind of emergency contemplated was not the kind we were facing at the moment. What had been contemplated was a forced landing or some similar occupationally related emergency in some remote area where high-level efforts would be required to get us out.

When Ron suddenly remembered the numbers, we all thought this would be the answer to our problem. Probably the numbers were for some military headquarters in each country and, if nothing else, through the local number we would be able to track down Captain Cardonas. Ron made another trip to the lobby desk. He spoke to the clerk and wrote down a number on a slip of paper which the clerk handed to the telephone operator. Suddenly a big flap developed. Ron headed back toward us across the lobby leaving the clerk and the telephone operator babbling at each other and waving their arms around in the air.

"Guess what?" Ron said.

"I'm afraid to," Joe said.

"Who do you think this number is for?"

"President Somoza," I said sarcastically.

"Well, smart-ass, that's exactly right."

"Oh, come on, Ron. Look, we've got to think of something. Did you call the number or not?"

"Hell no, I didn't call it. Look, I'm not kidding," Ron said. "This number is for the Nicaraguan White House."

"You'd *better* be kidding," Joe said.

"For Christ sake," I said. "This is like running out of money at the Mayflower bar and calling the White House to send somebody down to bail you out. We'd better call the Embassy."

"And who will we say we are?" Joe asked.

"Here comes the senior manager," Ron said.

The desk clerk was heading across the lobby. Captain Cardonas was on the phone. Ron explained the problem. Cardonas talked to the clerk, and in two minutes we were on the way to the airport in our taxi. We explained to Cardonas, or I thought we did, that the taxi driver was holding a tab and we didn't have enough money to pay him either. Cardonas walked over to the cab and screamed something to the driver in Spanish. I didn't see him give the driver any money, but the cab went rattling off at high speed toward town.

On the flight back to Puerto Cabezas, Cardonas came up forward to the cockpit. He was so highly scented it made our eyes water. He was also heavily powdered and rouged. He was a tall man who looked as if he were made entirely of fat and flab, no muscle.

Cardonas not only commanded the troops in his province, he was also the governor and the supreme court. Nicaragua was governed by a military dictatorship. Law enforcement in Puerto Cabezas, for instance, was handled not by a local police force but, instead, by rifle-toting members of the national army. Law violators appeared before Captain Cardonas for trial and sentencing. The owner of the "Green Front" bar in town told us that sometimes when Cardonas was in a bad mood, instead of sentencing a law violator to jail, he "banished" him. Banishment from Puerto Cabezas was not a simple matter of moving on down the road to the next town. There wasn't any road, and there wasn't any next town. When you arrived at the city limits of Puerto Cabezas, you were in the jungle. If a victim of Captain Cardonas' justice was not eaten alive by a jaguar, the aborigines probably used him as a pin cushion for their poison darts, or chopped his head off to shrink over a campfire. It was suggested that Cardonas was a fag. "He's nothing that straightforward," Gordon said. "Fatso is every kind of sexual aberrant that was ever invented, and some that haven't been."

Our last flight out of Puerto Cabezas departed for Miami on May 14. Bill flew the C-46. Burt rode copilot, and Ron and I mixed rum and Cokes in the back all the way to Miami.

We followed the usual course north through the Yucatan Channel into the Gulf of Mexico, and then east to Florida. Without making any conscious effort to keep track of our progress, some sixth sense told all of us in the back end when we were approaching the point that brought us closest to the western tip of Cuba. Almost as if on signal, conversations and gin rummy games stopped. Everyone stationed himself at a window, and we devoted the next 30 minutes to a careful and continuous scan of the skies.

Except for a small registry number on the vertical stabilizer, all of our aircraft were unmarked. They carried no airline, military or other identification. On flights to and from Miami we were sitting ducks if a Castro fighter came up to look us over and decided that he knew who we were and where we were coming from. This had happened on one occasion to Ernie on a return flight from Miami. He was flying at 9,000 feet above broken clouds when he spotted a single-engine fighter silhouetted against a towering cumulus. The fighter was climbing fast directly toward him from the direction of Cuba less than 90 miles away. The moment he spotted the fighter, Ernie chopped the throttles and dove toward the clouds below. In the clouds he reversed course and flew north for five minutes, then he headed west for 20 minutes before resuming his original heading. He didn't see the fighter again.

On our flight we were more apprehensive than usual. It was a clear day and there were no clouds to hide in. Bill said that he stayed a little west of course in order to give Cuba a wide berth. On a trip forward to the cockpit I saw the bright yellow display on the radar screen that was the west coast of Cuba. It was displayed on the screen at the 90-degree position. Bill pointed to the range mark. Cuba was 80 miles due east. I stood behind the two pilots and watched as the target moved down and off the screen. Riley, Pete, Wade and Leo lay somewhere on that island over the horizon.

I have heard us described as soldiers of fortune, spies, unemployed National Guard reservists and even as "swashbuckling, duplicitous, highhanded adventurers." There was no one in our group who even remotely fit any of those descriptions.

I didn't know Wade Gray before we were recruited for the operation. I didn't get to know him well afterwards. When we arrived in Central America, Wade was assigned to ground duties. His work was the maintenance, repair and installation of radio equipment. During the weeks we were in Florida I knew Wade as a man who was quiet, friendly and attentive to duty. He was a skilled aviation electronics specialist, a field that offers far greater opportunities than there are trained people to take advantage of them. Wade would never have become involved at the Bay of Pigs unless he had been specifically asked, and under circumstances where it was clear that the request for his services came from his own government. Wade was no "swashbuckling" adventurer or soldier of fortune. Except for the flight on Wednesday morning that cost him his life, he participated in no flight activities in Central America.

Riley Shamburger was big and beefy, and under the beef was muscle. He was gregarious, fun-loving and hell-raising. But Riley was no swaggering bravo. He was a highly-skilled test pilot. As a military pilot he was a squadron operations officer who inspired confidence, loyalty and affection from his men. He was one of those rare leaders who are genuinely concerned for the welfare and careers of his subordinates — and they knew it. Riley was actually not a member of our group.

Long before any of us were contacted, or knew anything about plans for the invasion at the Bay of Pigs, Riley was already into the planning of the operation at a Washington level. Where we were hired specifically to fly combat missions, Riley, by the nature and extent of his involvement, was specifically prohibited from flying. He was much too knowledgeable to risk having him fall into the hands of Castro. When Riley, Hal McGee, Vic and Connie were permitted to fly combat missions at the Bay of Pigs, it must have been with the full knowledge that capture and imprisonment were not among their options.

Leo Baker and I worked together often. He was flight engineer on many of the long flights out over the Pacific and across the mountains and jungles between Puerto Cabezas and Retalhuleu. We slept in side-by-side canvas cots in the tent where we lived alongside the runway at Puerto Cabezas, and we shared the penthouse at Retalhuleu.

Perhaps that is why I got to know Leo better than some of the other men. I got to know him well enough to learn that he was actually very few of the things he pretended to be. The man Leo pretended to be would not have lost his life at the Bay of Pigs. The man Leo pretended to be would not have been within 1,000 miles of the Bay of Pigs in the first place.

Leo was a short, dark, wiry little man in his mid-30s. He had jet black hair, an olive complexion, and dark brown eyes that mirrored a perpetual insolence. He was a difficult person to know and, for some, even harder to like. With a couple of beers under his belt he often became argumentative and combative. He talked in a loud voice and his vocabulary consisted almost entirely of four-letter words which he used fluently regardless of the company he was in. He got into fistfights with friends whom he goaded beyond endurance, and with strangers who were offended by his language and behavior.

On the surface Leo was a type easily recognized by anyone who has been in military service. There was one like him in every outfit. As far as

Leo was concerned, authority was his only real enemy. Discipline was designed purely and simply to shackle personal freedom. Rank to Leo was nothing more than a form of discrimination.

Leo was outspoken in his contempt for any expression of patriotism and love of country. Selflessness was a pose. Any human emotion that involved tenderness and compassion became a target for his scorn. Leo used his cynicism as a lance to puncture pretension, and to Leo, practically everyone was phony, or so he would have had you believe.

I began to learn some of the truth about Leo long before he was shot down on Wednesday morning. Until he remarried, shortly before he enlisted in our operation in Central America, Leo lived alone with a 12-year-old daughter in Birmingham. Leo was a flight test engineer at Hayes International, and he owned and managed a pizza shack near the airport on the side.

Every morning Leo's daughter made a lunch for Leo to take to work. She "kept house" for Leo with the help of a maid. As often as she could, she cooked dinner for Leo at night. Unless he was flying, they went to mass every Sunday.

I never asked Leo what personal family circumstances produced this situation. I only knew that he was divorced and had custody of his daughter. No doubt other arrangements were possible that would have placed far fewer restrictions on Leo's personal activities. As it was, and as he wanted it, Leo never let anything interfere with his responsibilities as a father. From many long talks with Leo in flight and in the tent where we lived at Puerto Cabezas, it became clear that Leo intended that nothing should ever separate the two. Leo, also, was not your typical "duplicitous, high-handed adventurer."

Once, while we were still in Ft. Lauderdale, Leo revealed a facet of his character entirely inconsistent with the image he tried to project. On occasion, Mac asked the flight engineers to stay behind after we landed from a flight to perform needed maintenance on the aircraft. Leo always griped loudly about this. He was explicit in his contempt for the professional abilities of the pilots, to whom he attributed any malfunction or breakdown.

One afternoon (on a day I had not been scheduled to fly) I returned to the apartment to be greeted by the news that Leo had been fired and was being sent back to Birmingham. It seems that he had been much too loud, and too vehement in his protests when Mac asked him to stay behind to work on the airplane. Later that afternoon I went across the street to say goodbye to Leo. I found him dressed in shorts and a T-shirt, drinking beer at the kitchen table, showing no evidence of imminent departure.

"I heard a rumor that you might be going back to Birmingham, Leo," I said cautiously.

"You've been listening to a lot of goddam gossip, Buck."

I didn't press the matter. Later Eric told me that Leo had called him on the phone, came to Eric's apartment and begged to be allowed to stay. To understand how difficult this must have been for Leo, you have to understand that Eric personified absolutely everything that Leo disliked about military rank, privilege and authority. At one point, according to Eric, Leo almost got down on his knees, offered to give up all his salary and work for nothing if Eric would allow him to go on to Central America with us.

The real truth about Leo was that all of his toughness and cynicism was a shield of some kind, but from what, I never quite figured out. I only know that down inside that hard-boiled egg there were some soft spots.

When Leo and Pete were hit on Wednesday morning they crashed on the airstrip at the Central Australia sugar plantation. From stories told later by civilians who lived on the plantation, it seems that Pete was badly injured in the crash and couldn't get out of the airplane. Leo, who was not seriously injured, jumped out of the plane with his .45 automatic in his hand, and was shot and killed by militia stationed in the area. Later, photographs found their way back to the United States that showed both Pete and Leo on the ground with bullet holes in their heads.

When I left the cockpit and went back into the cabin, I took a last look out the window, back over the sea towards Cuba. "Wherever you are now, you little bastard," I said to myself, "you won't have to hide behind that phony front anymore."

"If there's a law against hauling drunks in airplanes, I'll get life," Bill said when we landed in Miami. Strictly for his benefit, and Burt's, we continued the party at the Green Mansions Motel for another six hours.

Next day we were debriefed by company personnel. I caught a flight out of Miami late that night. On the way home from the airport in Birmingham I passed Leo's pizza shack. The windows were boarded up.

Postmortems

In the aftermath of the Bay of Pigs, public interest focused immediately on the causes for the failure of this adventure and who was to blame. It was the kind of issue that brought out the "crazies" at each end of the political spectrum. Accusations ranged all the way from assertions that "the Kennedys and the communists in the State Department" had deliberately sabotaged the invasion on orders from the Kremlin, to equally mad claims that the Pope had ordered President Kennedy to insure a Castro victory on grounds that Cuba is primarily a Catholic nation.

Some of the seeds sewn by this lunatic fringe were able to take root and grow — mostly because President Kennedy refused to provide a full report on the affair, and to let the chips fall wherever they may have.

At the top of the list of "crazies," the craziest of all had to have been the district attorney of New Orleans, Jim Garrison. In a protracted and highly publicized "investigation" of the role of the CIA in the assassination of President Kennedy, Garrison came up with the following sample of bizarre allegations:

- A number of men who killed the president were former employees of the CIA.
- He (a former member of the CIA) appeared at the home of friends in New Jersey, apparently badly shaken, and charged that Kennedy was killed by a small group within the CIA.
- From the moment the president's heart stopped beating, the agency attempted to sweep the whole conspiracy under the rug.
- Oswald was recruited by the CIA.
- A witness would be provided in court, a former CIA courier, who would testify to Oswald's CIA connections.
- There was a conspiracy by the CIA to conceal vital evidence from the Warren Commission.

Garrison offered this terrifying prognosis for the American people: "In a very real and terrifying sense," he said, "our government *is* the CIA. I've learned enough about the machinations of the CIA in the past year to know this is no longer the dream world America I once believed in."

The dream world occupied by Jim Garrison would be comical except that he was a person in a public position of considerable authority and responsibility. When he called a press conference on February 18, 1963, to launch his campaign against the CIA, media representatives from all over the world came to record and report his fantasies.

Beginning on Friday, April 28, 1961, less than ten days after the collapse of the invasion, a subcommittee of the Senate Committee on Foreign Affairs began its postmortem examination of the Bay of Pigs fiasco.

The subcommittee interrogated and took testimony from CIA Director Allen Dulles, Secretary of State Dean Rusk, and Chairman of the Joint Chiefs of Staff Lyman Lemnitzer, among others. Over a period of three weeks, 317 pages of testimony was transcribed. The committee held all of its hearings in "executive" session, which means that its final report was classified and thus unavailable to the public.

It is not clear, therefore, what purpose was intended to have been served by this Senate investigation, other than to satisfy the curiosity of the individual members of the committee and some of their colleagues in the Senate. The transcript of these hearings reveals absolutely nothing that would compromise the security of the United States (discounting the possible ridicule of the Senate committee itself). A careful study of the committee report reveals much more about the committee itself than it does about the Bay of Pigs.

An inordinate amount of time was wasted by the Senators in flowery exchanges of the mutual regard and high esteem in which each held all the others, and the high regard and admiration of the entire committee for all the witnesses who appeared before it. After tossing these posies around in every session, the committee failed completely to discover (a) what had happened and, (b) why.

Individual committee members were constantly late arriving at the hearings, and missed much of the witnesses' testimony, or they were under constant pressure to rush from the hearings to take care of more pressing business elsewhere. It is doubtful if any single member of the committee heard *all* of the questions and *all* of the answers.

The witnesses themselves were less than forthcoming. They volunteered nothing. The committee never learned, for instance, of the last minute decisions by the president that altered the concept and the conduct of the original operational plan.

They heard nothing about Trinidad. They did not discover why air strikes had been severely restricted. When attribution to "higher authority" was made by witnesses, the senators failed to grasp the fact that the only authority higher than that of the people they were talking to was the president himself. Committee members invariably failed to react to the potential for follow-up that many of their questions generated. For instance:

> *Senator Morse:* Did we supply them with planes at all?
>
> *Secretary Rusk:* I think they were supplied planes for their own small air force, their very own.
>
> *Senator Morse:* Flown by Cuban refugees?
>
> *Secretary Rusk:* Yes sir. I do understand that there was an American soldier of fortune who, without authorization, so far as policy is concerned, was involved in one of these planes.
>
> *Senator Morse:* Would there be any basis in fact for the vicious communist propaganda that to any extent there were American volunteers involved in the episode?
>
> *Secretary Rusk:* Well, there were in Guatemala. But I would have to ask you to confirm this with Mr. Dulles when you see him.
>
> *Senator Morse:* I will come back. I have some other policy questions that I wanted to ask, but I raised these questions that would help direct the discussion a bit, and I will turn to my colleague, Senator Sparkman.
>
> *Senator Sparkman:* Mr. Chairman, I came in late. I am sorry. I had a speaking engagement. I will not ask any questions, but I am sure this has been covered quite well.

The above exchange is quite typical of the committee gobbledy-gook. The only thing of any potential substance that emerged was Secretary of State Rusk's statement that there may have been one American "soldier of fortune" who was involved without authorization. The truth is, of course, that Secretary Rusk was much better informed than he permitted any of his testimony to reveal.

On Tuesday, May 2, CIA Director Allen Dulles, and Deputy Director Richard Bissel appeared before the Senate committee.

> *Senator Long:* Do you feel that the planning of this operation failed to anticipate that there would be air opposition from the Castro forces by at least as much as six aircraft?
>
> *Mr. Bissel:* No sir. Our information beforehand on the numbers and location of Castro aircraft, I think, was proved out in the event. I think it has to be said that in an operation of this character there are always conflicting considerations. There is, on the one hand, a desire to achieve the greatest possible effectiveness, in this case military effectiveness. There is, on the other hand the desire to preserve the purely Cuban character of the operation and its appearance as an operation that the Cubans might well have run on their own. These two considerations influenced a number of decisions concerning the execution of the operation.
>
> I think with hindsight that there could have been a more effective use of airpower at certain points. . . . I do not say this with intent, with an implication of criticism. I mean to emphasize the fact that in the weighing of the two sets of considerations I have referred to, decisions of this sort are made.

In this response, Mr. Bissel said that more effective use of air power could have been made "at certain points" but that there were two conflicting sets of consdierations involved, political and military, and that these two considerations influenced a number of decisions concerning the execution of the operation. Senator Long did not follow up this opening by asking what the considerations were, how they affected the operation, and who made the decisions. His next question was about landing craft.

The Senate committee did not penetrate one inch beyond the stone wall erected by the witnesses they questioned, and it is apparent from reading the transcript of the hearings that they did not even recognize the existence of the wall.

Chairman of the Joint Chiefs of Staff Lyman Lemnitzer appeared before the committee on Friday, May 19.

> *Senator Symington:* What do you mean by an air strike that failed?
> *General Lemnitzer:* They had what fighters we had information about; their bombers were located on three fields. These fields were to be hit by the Cuban Air Force at approximately daylight on D-day. This did not go.
> *Senator Capehart:* When you say "Cuban" you mean the revolutionary forces?
> *General Lemnitzer:* Revolutionary forces.
> *Senator Capehart:* They were to hit the three airports on the morning?
> *General Lemnitzer:* That is right.
> *Senator Capehart:* And they did not go?
> *General Lemnitzer:* It was abandoned.
> *Senator Capehart:* They did not fly?
> *General Lemnitzer:* They did not make those attacks.
> *Senator Capehart:* Do you know why?
> *General Lemnitzer:* No, I do not know why.

General Lemnitzer did know why. On the day before, May 18, he had testified before the committee of inquiry headed by General Maxwell Taylor to the effect that the had been informed at two o'clock in the morning on D-day that the president had cancelled the D-day air strikes.

On April 22, 1961, President Kennedy appointed a committee to study governmental practices and programs in the area of paramilitary, guerrilla, and antiguerrilla activity, which fell short of outright war, with a view to strengthening our work in that area. The president directed special attention to the lessons which could be learned from the Bay of Pigs.

As submitted to the president, the committee's report focused almost exclusively on the Bay of Pigs, an affair which had cost the president heavily in personal prestige and credibility in the early months of his administration.

The findings of the committee were immediately classified and therefore served no useful purpose as a means of providing information concerning this event to the general public. Twenty years later, in compliance with the directives of the Public Information Act, a heavily sanitized copy of the committee's report was released from the Kennedy archives at Harvard University. In the form released, many lines of testimony are deleted; two entire sessions of the hearings are deleted, and names of most witnesses are deleted.

In a careful study of this report, I discovered several errors in facts of which I had personal, firsthand knowledge. I could find no plausible explanation for these errors. I also found it almost impossible to identify these witnesses from their testimony. Although names of witnesses were deleted from the transcripts, I should have been able to identify those whom I had known, and who were testifying on subjects concerning which I had personal knowledge. Puzzlingly, I could not.

There was one witness whom I could identify from his testimony because of the highly specialized and unique activities in which he was engaged prior to the force landing on Monday morning. I tracked this witness down and described my problem with this report in the hope that he would have a logical explanation for some of the glaring discrepancies I have discovered in the transcript. He said, "I understand how you could recognize the remarks attributed to me. But what you don't know is that I, myself, could hardly recognize my own testimony when I read this report. It was edited."

Here then, was evidence to go along with my own, that what I had anticipated would be an accurate historical document (at last!) was, in fact, seriously flawed. An even more careful analysis reinforced this judgment, and established new doubts.

In its report, the committee provided no information on who had selected the witnesses or how they were qualified. It may be more important to know who did not testify than who did. For instance, Colonel Hal McGee did not testify. Yet Hal functioned at a command post level in Washington, at an operational command level in Central America, and he actually flew the mission on Wednesday, April 19. It is difficult to understand why Hal would not have been among the witnesses called to testify.

On the other hand, General Doster did testify. Yet Reid Doster was not briefed on as high a level as Hal McGee and Riley Shamburger. Doster, for instance, had never set foot in the command post in Washington.

The committee decided at its first session not to tape the hearings but to use recording secretaries from the Joint Staff. These reporters were sometimes present, and sometimes not. They did not make verbatim records of the hearings. They took notes. From these notes they prepared and edited a record at the end of the day. Although in format the transcripts appear to be verbatim, in fact, they are not. They are reports prepared from the notes made by the reporters and, according to their own disclaimer "represent only the general substance of the statements made." This explains how a mission flown on Tuesday night by six American contract pilots got into the record (no such mission was ever flown), and why one witness had a hard time recognizing his own testimony.

There is no way of knowing whether, or how much, President Kennedy may have hoped that the committee's investigation and report would get him off the hook. That it did not serve this purpose must be imputed from his refusal to make it public. Remember, there was no longer any hope whatever that the United States government's participation at the Bay of Pigs could be concealed, only details and decisions that led to its failure remained to be covered up.

There were two people who had intimate, personal knowledge of these details and decisions: Admiral Arleigh Burke because of the Navy's role and potential involvement, and CIA Director Allen Dulles whose agency had formulated the plans and directed the operation from beginning to end.

When President Kennedy appointed Arleigh Burke and Allen Dulles to the investigating committee, he effectively silenced the two people who could have commented on the Bay of Pigs with more knowledge and authority than anyone else in Washington. Whether President Kennedy made these appointments with that in mind is, of course, pure speculation.

General Maxwell Taylor retired from the Army as its Chief of Staff. He joined Kennedy's White House staff as the president's chief military adviser. Following the completion of his assignment as chairman of the Bay of Pigs committee of inquiry, President Kennedy appointed him Chairman of the Joint Chiefs of Staff.

Attorney General Robert Kennedy, the president's brother, was the fourth member of the committee.

The characters and reputations of General Taylor, Admiral Burke, and Mr. Dulles are too well-established to support speculation that any of them would contribute to the whitewash of the Bay of Pigs. In fact the committee's summary report detailing the "Causes of Failure of Operation Zapata" by no means absolves the president of his responsibility for the failure of the operation, quite the contrary. But by meticulously avoiding specific reference to the president, the president's specific, personal contribution to the defeat of the Cuban expeditionary force was made quite obscure.

In memorandum number 3, paragraph 1 (b), setting forth the conclusions of the Cuban study group, the report says: "Once the need for the operation was established, its success should have had the primary consideration of all agencies of the government. Operational restrictions designed to protect its character should have been accepted only if they did not impair the chance of success. As it was, the leaders of the operation were obliged to fit their plan inside changing ground rules laid down for non-military considerations, which often had serious operational disadvantages."

In identifying "Immediate Causes of Failure of the Operation," the committee found that these causes rested on

> ...the attitude toward it on the part of government officials. The effectiveness of the Castro air force over the beach resulted from a failure to destroy the airplanes on the ground before or concurrently with the landing.
>
> This failure was a consequence of the restraints put on the anti–Castro air force in planning and executing its strikes, primarily for the purpose of protecting the covert character of the operation. Those restraints included: the limitation of prelanding strikes to those which could be flown from non–U.S. controlled airfields under the guise of coming from Cuban strips; the prohibition of the use of American contract pilots for tactical air operations; restrictions on ammunition, notably napalm; and the cancellation of the strikes planned at dawn on D-day.
>
> The last mentioned was probably the most serious as it eliminated the last favorable opportunity to destroy the Castro air force on the ground. The cancellation seems to have resulted partly from the failure to make the air strike plan clear in advance to the president and the secretary of state, but, more importantly, by misgivings as to the effect of the air strikes on the position of the United States in the current U.N. debate on Cuba.

The Taylor Committee described accurately the reasons for the failure of the invasion effort, but it did not make clear that the policies, "ground rules," and specific decisions were those of the president, not the CIA and the military. The committee was wrong in a statement that

> While the Joint Chiefs of Staff supported the Trinidad plan as one having a fair chance of success, the plan encountered difficulties in other quarters. From its inception the plan had been developed under ground rules that it must remain covert in character, that is, it should include no action which, if revealed, could not be plausibly denied by the United States and should look to the world as an operation exclusively conducted by the Cubans.

This was by no means a ground rule that had existed from inception but had, in fact been laid down by President Kennedy late in the game.

A study of the Taylor Committee report, with its obvious flaws and errors, and more particularly the appearance of a measure of restraint in its language, suggests that General Taylor, Admiral Burke and Mr. Dulles may have "tilted" in a direction that would protect the president from having to suffer some of the consequences that may have followed too great exposure of his timidity and irresolution at the Bay of Pigs. Furthermore, I have the idea (because it has been suggested to me by a credible source) that Arleigh Burke and Allen Dulles — and perhaps Maxwell Taylor — felt a measure of sympathy for a young president, new on the job, and they believed that their more experienced shoulders were broad enough to help him absorb some of the burden created by the Bay of Pigs.

Timidity, irresolution and indecisiveness can result in serious errors in judgment. President Kennedy demonstrated this at the Bay of Pigs. Bad judgment, however, is not a crime — particularly if you have not yet gotten a real good handle on your new job. What is inexcusable is to create all the consequences of poor judgment and wrong decisions, and deliberately and purposefully shift the responsibility to someone else. By transferring responsibility for the failure of the mission at the Bay of Pigs to the CIA and the military strategists at the Pentagon, and by covering up his own role in this unfortunate event, President Kennedy could, and did, inspire the kind of diatribe indulged in by Senator Stephen Young of Ohio. In the multi-million-circulation national periodical *Playboy*, Senator Young launched an attack in defense of the president with statements like these:

- "The CIA is not satisfied to be our watchdog, but wants to be its own master. It has taken on the character of a second government, answerable to no one."
- "The Bay of Pigs invasion of Cuba was an object lesson in an international political failure. It was appalling to learn how all the signals were confounded — the lack of coordination, the waste of manpower, the failure to provide the promised umbrella of bombers over the beaches as the Cuban freedom fighters made their landing."
- "The late President Kennedy gallantly took the blame for the Bay of Pigs disaster, but it was plain by that time how disgracefully faulty had been the information he had been given before the April 1961, landings, how mismanaged the whole affair was from beginning to end, largely by CIA bungling."
- "The CIA not only deceived the president in this case, the people of the United States were also deceived, and quite deliberately."

Senator Young, of course, didn't know what he was talking about. But this violent attack on the CIA by a senior member of the United States Senate could only have been made possible by the successful effort to withhold from him information he should have had; and by an effort, also successful, to create the fictions that Senator Young accepted as gospel because of their source.

For almost two years following the unsuccessful invasion attempt at the Bay of Pigs, an impression was allowed to take root and grow that the invasion had failed because of last-minute decisions by President Kennedy to cancel previously planned U.S. air support for the invading forces.

If such a decision had been made, it would have been entirely consistent with President Kennedy's often repeated statements that under no circumstances would the United States government intervene militarily in the affairs of the Cuban government. The conflict, as the president pointed out only four days before the invasion was launched, was not between the United States and Cuba, but between Cubans and Cubans.

The fact is, no such decision was made. No such decision was ever necessary. There had never been any plan to use United States air forces in the invasion in the first place. Nevertheless, it became widely accepted that lack of United States military air support at the Bay of Pigs was a result of this policy decision by the president.

This was the view held by a group of newspaper editors who met with the president on May 10, 1961. It was the view held by most members of Congress, and by most of the general public. For a long time no official reference was ever made to the intended role in the invasion of the exile group's *own* air force — or even that such an air force had existed.

In Birmingham, in 1962, I became managing editor of a metropolitan weekly newspaper, *The Examiner*. With a growing feeling of disenchantment and a sense of wonder, I followed the scuffling around in high places to get the story straight on the Bay of Pigs.

Finally, I decided to write a story, my own postmortem, for *The Examiner*. In doing so, I had three main objectives in mind. One was to make public the fact that the Cuban invasion forces had gone ashore at the Bay of Pigs at the mercy, and under the guns, of the Castro air force because the president had denied permission at the last minute for the exiles to strike at Castro's air bases and destroy his combat aircraft on the ground.

Another was to point out that concerted efforts in Washington to shift responsibilty for the failure of the invasion to the CIA amounted to nothing more than high-level buck-passing.

My third reason for publishing this story concerned the wives and families of the four men who had lost their lives at the Bay of Pigs.

The deaths of Riley, Pete, Leo and Wade created a problem for the government. Their disappearance had to be explained. Then too, there was the matter of the insurance we had all taken out at the time we signed our contracts.

The cover story devised, and relayed to the families of the four flyers, was that all four men had been employed by a group of wealthy Cubans. According to this story, the men had been lost in the crash of a cargo plane in flight between Miami and Central America.

The "Cubans" who employed the four airmen had provided life insurance and had set up a trust fund which would provide each of the widows with a lifetime income of $550 per month. This story was also given to the press. Newspapers quoted a representative of the "Cuban" group as saying that "the men knew what they were getting into and would have had a nice little nest egg if they had gotten back."

The government had to provide a cover story and perhaps this is the best they could come up with on short notice. There were several things about the way this affair was handled, however, that spelled trouble. In Birmingham many of the activities of our people were an open secret. There was no knowledge of precise details, but among friends, associates and families, there was little doubt that Riley, Pete, Leo and Wade had been killed during the invasion at the Bay of Pigs.

Such speculation was all well and good for friends and acquaintances, but what the widows and children were told, in effect, was that their husbands and fathers, with heavy family responsibilities, had somehow been persuaded to go off on a harebrained adventure for purely monetary gain, and had lost their lives in the process, leaving behind families who would have to face the future as the doubtful beneficiaries of an anonymous group of wealthy Cubans. True, the monthly checks began to arrive from a New York bank, but there was never anything in hand to show that a contractual obligation existed, nothing that any of them could borrow a nickel on to finance a child's education, or to pay for a costly illness, or to buy a home.

I mailed the complete text of my story to Attorney General Robert Kennedy several weeks in advance of its publication. When the paper was published I mailed copies to every member of Congress. I received no acknowledgment from the attorney general, but during the last week in January 1963, he arranged an interview with David Kraslow of the Knight newspaper chain.

In this interview, and in a subsequent interview with *U.S. News and World Report*, Robert Kennedy volunteered that the president had never reneged on a promise to supply U.S. Navy jets at the Bay of Pigs for the reason that no such promise nor any such plans had ever been made. The attorney general said the invaders "got all the air cover the plan called for" and he said that the fact that "there was not sufficient air cover at the beach was one of several major mistakes" responsible for the failure to liberate Cuba.

"The plan that was used," Kennedy said, "was cleared by the CIA and the Joint Chiefs of Staff. It was programmed at the Pentagon in whatever manner they do these things."

Although he never explained why he did it, the revival of the Bay of Pigs issue by Attorney General Kennedy in 1963 created a storm in Congress. It could not have been lost on members of Congress that his reopening of the question coincided with the distribution of my newspaper at the Capital.

Senator Goldwater told the Senate that the Kennedy administration should make public all official reports on the invasion, and that the administration should end its efforts to tamper with history. Senator Dirksen proposed making a preliminary inquiry of his own. Other senators proposed a Senate investigation to get the entire story historically correct.

President Kennedy, who was usually quite articulate, found it difficult to speak coherently on the Bay of Pigs. On January 24, 1963, the following exchange took place at the president's press conference at the White House:

> *Question:* There seem to be questions on the part of history involving the Bay of Pigs invasion. As you know, the attorney general says that no United States air support was contemplated so therefore there was none to be withdrawn. Yet today editor Jack Gore of the *Ft. Lauderdale News* says that in a group of editors who visited with you on May 10, 1961, you recalled then the air cover was available but you had decided not to use it. Mr. Gore says you told these editors that one reason for your decision was that Ambassador Stevenson had complained that any such action would make a liar out of you in the UN. Now there is a wealth of seemingly different stories and I am wondering if you could set us straight on what the real situation was?

President Kennedy's reply was incoherent:

> Yes, there was no United States air cover planned, and so that the first part of the statement attributed to the attorney general is correct. What was talked about was the question of an air strike on Monday morning by planes which were flown by — our B-26s — which were flown by pilots based in — not in the United States, not American planes. That strike, as the attorney general's interview in *U.S. News and World Report* describes it, was postponed until Monday afternoon.
>
> I think members of the Brigade were under the impression that the planes which were available were the B-26 planes and would give them protection on the beaches. That did not work out. That was one of the failures — the jets, the training jets, which were used against them were very effective, and, therefore, we were not — the Brigade was not able to maintain air supremacy on the beach so I think that the confusion comes from the use of the word air cover.
>
> Let's talk about United States air cover as opposed to air cover from — which was attached to the Brigade, some of which flew from various parts of the continent not from the United States, so that, therefore, as I said from the beginning, the operation was a failure and that the responsibility rests with the White House.

Members of Congress were far from satisfied. (How could they have been otherwise?) Senator Goldwater pointed out that "there was no denial from the White House nor from the attorney general, when stories were printed throughout the nation that air cover was withheld on orders of the president. They should have left it alone. It is a black blot on American history."

Senator Morse suggested to members of the Senate that they could get the answers to questions raised by Senator Goldwater by reading the secret testimony taken by his subcommittee.

Goldwater said that he had read it and it was "the most inconclusive testimony I have ever had the pleasure to read." Senator Goldwater demanded a full-scale investigation by the Senate Armed Services Committee.

Senator Richard B. Russell, chairman of the Armed Services Committee said it was up to the committee members to decide if such an investigation would serve a useful purpose. Senator Russell also questioned the wisdom of the attorney general in rehashing the episode in newspapers and magazines. He said he found it "a little difficult to see what the attorney general — even if he is the president's brother — had to do with the Bay of Pigs in his official capacity."

At about this time Eugene S. Pulliam, managing editor of the Indianapolis *News*, and chairman of the Freedom of Information Committee of the American Society of Newspaper Editors, wrote to the Society's chairman, Turner Catledge of the *New York Times*. Mr. Pulliam said in his letter, "We honestly feel that much information is being withheld not for security reasons, but to protect individuals in the mistaken belief that what the people don't know won't hurt them."

What revived much more widespread interest in the Bay of Pigs were two stories I wrote for Chicago's *American*. General David Hutchinson, a regular Air Force officer, and General Doster's immediate superior, told the *American* that General Doster was the man they should talk to if they wanted to learn anything about the Bay of Pigs because, General Hutchinson said, General Doster had been in charge. Of course General Doster had not been in charge, but when the *American* contacted him, Doster referred them to me. The result was that the story that had appeared in the *Examiner* on February 3, 1963, appeared in Chicago's *American* on March 7 and was followed by another front page story on March 8.

The circulation of the *American* was somewhat larger than that of the *Examiner*, to say the least. Consequently the national news media quickly learned that four Americans had been shot down in combat at the Bay of Pigs. This seemed to be what interested the press the most. I did not believe this was the main issue. Some of our people could have been killed no matter what the circumstances. But I felt that something worthwhile had been accomplished when President Kennedy was asked a question at a news conference in March to which he made this reply:

> Let me say this about these four men. The flight that cost them their lives was a voluntary flight, and that because of the nature of their work it has not been a matter of public record, as it might be in the case of soldiers or sailors, I can say that they were serving their country.

I don't know how much pain and anguish this may have caused the president. I would like to think none at all. And I think it is great, and I hope that he did, too, that the children of the four flyers who lost their lives at the Bay of Pigs can be proud in the knowledge that their dads did not run off and leave them just to chase some will-o'-the-wisp, but that they died in the service of their country. They know this is true because the president of the United States himself acknowledged it.

The invasion of Cuba at the Bay of Pigs was staged from Puerto Cabezas in Nicaragua. Troop and supply ships sailed from Puerto Cabezas. Air support for the invasion was launched from Puerto Cabezas, and I and the other airmen from Birmingham were based at Puerto Cabezas as active participants throughout the entire period. Based on our own eyewitness observations of events at the time, and on the spot, backed up by the testimony of people at the highest level of operational command, the conclusion is inescapable: The failure of the invasion at the Bay of Pigs was due primarily to the timidity, irresolution and indecisiveness of President Kennedy and his administration.

In the aftermath, the conclusion is equally inescapable that to conceal his culpability, President Kennedy not only permitted, he assisted in shifting the responsibility to the CIA.

The CIA has never fully recovered from the damage inflicted on it by President Kennedy at the time of the Bay of Pigs. The word "cover-up" was not coined until much later, but it could have been appropriately applied to Kennedy's efforts to salvage his reputation and personal status at that time. The president took full, personal responsibility, of course, which is standard procedure for the top man in such situations. For the most part, but not entirely, he left it to others in his administration to provide the raw material to journalists and other observers of the times who wanted to investigate and report on the event in detail.

One of the first books to appear was *The Invisible Government*, written by David Wise and Thomas Ross. David Wise is a native New Yorker and a graduate of Columbia University. He joined the New York *Herald Tribune* in 1951, and moved to the paper's Washington bureau in 1958. After the 1960 presidential election, he was named the newspaper's White House correspondent. He became chief of his newspaper's Washington bureau in 1963.

Thomas B. Ross is a graduate of Yale. He served as a junior officer in the Navy during the Korean War. He subsequently worked for the International News Service and for United Press International. In 1958 he became a member of the Washington bureau of the Chicago *Sun Times*.

As youthful as the president and most of his staff was, and with the same Ivy League backgrounds, it may not be unfair to suggest that Wise and Ross benefited in their research by somewhat better access to White

House sources, on friendlier terms, than otherwise may have occurred. That they did have access to high-level sources is obvious from their book. That what they wrote almost borders on fiction must be explained, then, in some other way.

The Invisible Government account of the Bay of Pigs invasion consists of four chapters in an overall story of United States intelligence and espionage. On the book's dust jacket the publishers (Random House) say:

> This startling and disturbing book is the first full authentic account of America's intelligence apparatus — an Invisible Government with the CIA at its center, that conducts clandestine policies of the United States in the Cold War. The invisible government is made up of many agencies and people ... but the largest and most important of all is the Central Intelligence Agency. Four important chapters concentrate on the Bay of Pigs: disclosing the CIA's intricate but doomed plan for the operation and how the cover story failed; what was behind the controversy over the question of air cover.

The authors attribute the failure of the invasion primarily to decisions which became necessary when it began to look as if a certain cover story would unravel. This was the story about the Cuban pilot, Captain Zúñiga, who flew a B-26 (shot full of holes on the ramp at Puerto Cabezas) to Miami on Saturday morning, April 15.

Zúñiga landed at Miami's municipal airport with one prop feathered. This was just window dressing. He had shut the engine down a few miles out from the field. Zúñiga's story was that he and other Cuban pilots had revolted against Castro and had attacked various fields in Cuba that morning. These attacks, of course, had been accomplished by the first mission flown from Puerto Cabezas.

This incredible incident was staged as a part of the effort by President Kennedy to conceal our participation in the attack on Cuba. It was unbelievably naive. Castro himself would know that Cuban pilots had not made the attacks on the airfields from those same airfields. As for the rest of the world, what was necessary for credible denial of United States involvement was that the mission to overthrow Castro must succeed, not fail. President Kennedy's massive, last-minute revision of the operational plans had already eliminated that possibility.

If The Invisible Government was intended to have been a "voice" for administration explanations of what went wrong at the Bay of Pigs, then what we were asked to believe was that the Cuban invasion force was simply *defeated* by basic weaknesses in the planning and execution of a military operation which was more or less doomed from the start, and which began and ended when the invaders went ashore and discovered that they were up against a too-powerful adversary and overwhelming odds.

This is exactly the theme that is emphasized by Wise and Ross in their reconstruction of events at the Bay of Pigs. Those of us who were there are left to resolve as best we can the conflict between what Wise and Ross were told by their high-level sources, and what we actually observed.

During the course of his research for *The Invisible Government*, David Wise came to Birmingham to interview me. He had read the two stories I wrote for Chicago's *American*. I repeated to Wise what I had said in the two newspaper stories. Wise was not particularly interested. I didn't know it at the time, of course, but he already had what he considered to be much more authoritative information on what had transpired at the Bay of Pigs. Wise was interested in getting the names of men who had participated in the invasion. I explained that I could not reveal the names of men involved for obvious reasons. Some of them may still have been involved in activities that could be compromised if they were identified with the Bay of Pigs.

Even so, Wise insisted on putting a list of names of people on the table between us, and requesting that I identify them if I could. I could, but I didn't. However, I did make note of the fact that the list included the names of men who very definitely had been in Guatemala and Nicaragua — including Larry, Al and Frank. Even more interesting, he had last names to go with the first names. I had only known these people by their first names. Later, I was able to confirm that the last names on Wise's list were the phonies used by Larry, Al and Frank — which means that David Wise really *did* have access to files at incredibly high and top secret levels.

In their book, Wise and Ross begin their account by citing "heavy losses on the Saturday raid." In fact, there was only one aircraft lost. And according to these authors, "The CIA plans hinged on the assumption that Zuniga's cover story would hold up for at least 48 hours. In that event, the second strike would seem like the work of rebelling Cuban pilots." (Where were these "rebelling pilots" and their aircraft supposed to hole up for two days?)

Actually, a second strike was planned for Saturday afternoon as a follow-up to the attack on the air bases that morning. Another strike was planned for Sunday morning. It, too, was a vital part of the operation. It was to have been launched against a large concentration of Castro's armored equipment gathered in a staging area in a field beside the Cuban Military Academy. (I saw the reconnaissance photo used to establish this target.)

The next strike was scheduled for Monday morning, again at air bases to insure the complete destruction of Castro's combat aircraft, and to take out microwave communications stations, power plants and military installations. All of these strikes were cancelled.

Attorney General Robert Kennedy referred to the Monday mission as the planned "second" strike. In an interview with *U.S. News and World*

Report he said: "There was supposed to be another attack on the airfields on Monday morning, and in fact it took place later that day."

It did not.

In the CIA/military plan, control of the air was vital to the success of the operation. It had been planned for and was obtainable, even as late as Monday morning. Air superiority was not achieved, and the expeditionary force and its supply ships were left at the mercy of Castro's aircraft which had survived Saturday's pared down raid.

It was not the CIA's plan that was unravelling at the edges, but the president's.

At one point in their description of air actions at the Bay of Pigs, Wise and Ross describe a pilot looking at his watch as his aircraft crosses the beach. It is eleven-fifteen. At two-fifteen, they say, the bomber turned for home. This checking of watches and noting of precise timing, right down to the minute, lend the Wise and Ross account a certain authenticity, almost as if they were transcribing entries from an actual mission log. However, even though Wise and Ross are not pilots, they are investigative journalists. With a little checking, they could have learned that it was impossible for a B-26 to fly from Nicaragua to Cuba, stooge around for three hours, and get back home. And if they were not curious about fuel capacity and range, they could have wondered how a B-26 could carry enough armament — bombs, rockets and 50-calibre ammo — to last for three hours. Maybe to the authors these discrepancies were not relevant to the desired thrust of their story — if they noticed them at all — but they should have aroused maybe, just a faint suspicion that some of the stuff they were being fed was not credible. And it wasn't.

The authors describe a mission of six aircraft which took off at two o'clock on Tuesday afternoon. "Two bombers," they say, "were flown by American CIA pilots." Six bombers did not take off on Tuesday afternoon. There was a six-aircraft mission that did take off before dawn on Tuesday morning. No Americans were on that mission.

Wise and Ross also say that on Wednesday morning the president authorized unmarked Navy jets from the carrier *Essex* to fly over the beach for one hour just before dawn. Somewhere along the line there was a fatal mix-up between the Navy and the CIA. In secret postmortems over the Bay of Pigs, it was officially concluded that the bombers had arrived after the jets had already come and gone, after the hour had run out on the hour of air support.

In other words, according to Wise and Ross, the Navy fighters were launched from the carrier in darkness, flew a one-hour patrol over the beach in darkness, and returned to the carrier before the B-26s arrived at dawn to perform their mission.

There was no "mix-up." The Navy fighters were there. Two of them escorted Don Gordon off the beach. Another sent a Castro Sea Fury scuttling for cover.

The Invisible Government made a significant, if unwitting, contribution to the cover-up. It was a best seller, a Book-of-the-Month Club selection, and it was read by thousands of Americans.

Two other lengthy and equally "authoritative" accounts of the Bay of Pigs appeared in this same time period. These also established that the invasion failed in spite of sustained efforts by weary crews who "flew around the clock" to support the hard-pressed troops on the beach—"losing six of eleven planes on D-day alone in the process."

Decision for Disaster, "at last the truth about the Bay of Pigs," was a feature length article in the September 1964, *Reader's Digest*. It was written by Dr. Mario Lazo, a Havana attorney "whose international connections in high places," according to *Reader's Digest*, "made it possible for him to speak in confidence with those who knew what happened in Washington during those critical days in April."

Dr. Lazo may have learned what happened in Washington, but he most certainly did not learn what happened in Nicaragua. Dr. Lazo was told by his "connections in high places" that the B-26s flew almost continual relays until, on Wednesday, April 19, "a final mission was pieced together."

Dr. Lazo says that by Wednesday morning only three flyable aircraft were left at Puerto Cabezas—two B-26s and a C-46. These last two B-26s were shot down, says Dr. Lazo.

The Bay of Pigs is the title of a book written by Haynes Johnson in collaboration with four of the Brigade's leaders, Manuel Artime, José Pérez San Román, Erneido Oliva and Enrique Ruiz-Williams. *The Bay of Pigs* is also billed as "at long last the truth about the Bay of Pigs invasion of Cuba." It purports to give "the inside story of what really went on at the White House meetings where the agony of decision was endured . . . and in the councils of the CIA and the Pentagon. . . . In all and in detail, it is a heroic tale and a shocking revelation. His information comes from unimpeachable sources."

Mr. Johnson and his collaborators, leaders of the expeditionary force, describe sensational events. The invasion was going to take place even if Washington decided to call it off. The authors say that near the end of March, the CIA official in charge of their training in Guatemala called Artime aside one day and told him that there were "forces in the administration trying to block the invasion," and that it might be called off.

"If this happens, you come here and make some kind of show, as if you are putting us, the advisers, in prison, and you go ahead with the program as we have talked about it, and we will give you the whole plan, even if we are your prisoners."

According to Johnson the CIA official was quite specific. The brigade leaders were instructed that they were to place an armed guard at each American's door, cut communications to the outside world, and continue the training until he told when and how to leave for "Trampoline" base. "In the end," he laughed, "we will win."

This story stetches credulity to the breaking point. The "CIA official" referred to was a high ranking officer in the U.S. Marine Corps. What Johnson and his four Cuban collaborators ask their readers to believe is that this officer proposed a course of action for which he could not only have been cashiered from the service, but sent to prison. Whether it is intended or not, since this American conspirator was identified as a "CIA official," the story does serious discredit to the CIA in the eyes of anyone who accepts it at face value.

In spite of Johnson's competence as a reporter, and the technical qualifications of his collaborators, *The Bay of Pigs* suffers in more ways than one from a lack of credibility. It is understandable that the four Cubans who collaborated in writing the book would have a high regard and warm personal feelings for Robert Kennedy. After all, the attorney general was largely responsible for putting together the ransom deal that got them sprung from prison in Cuba. As a probable consequence, their book comes across as more of a propaganda piece for Kennedy than as an objective account of the events it describes. In many ways it reads as if it may have been written on the lawn at Hickory Hill in McLean, Virginia — which, I have been told, it was.

Theodore Sorensen, a longtime personal friend of President Kennedy, and a member of his White House staff from the beginning, deals at length with the Bay of Pigs and the CIA in his book about the Kennedy period. Sorensen believes, as he says the president believed, that Kennedy was virtually betrayed by the CIA. According to Sorensen, it was a tragic error for the president to have ever put his faith and trust in this agency in the first place!

> The President was told that the use of the exile brigade would make possible the toppling of Castro, without actual aggression by the United States, without seeming to outsiders to violate the principles of non-intervention, with no risk of involvement and with little risk of failure.
> Could the exile brigade achieve its goals without our participation? He was assured in writing that it could — a wild misjudgment.
> Were the members of the exile brigade willing to risk this effort without our military participation, the President asked, and go ahead with the realization that we would not intervene if they failed? He was assured that they were — a serious misstatement, due at least in part to bad communications on the part of the CIA liaison officers.

Sorensen describes the B-26s employed by the exile brigade as "lumbering, slow, and unwieldy; unsuited to air cover." He says that the initial air strike against Castro's air bases was ineffective and that "as a result the president was urged on Sunday by his foreign policy advisers – but without a formal meeting at which the military and CIA could be heard – to call off the Monday morning strike. The president concurred in that conclusion. The second strike was cancelled."

In summing up, Sorensen says:

> The first strike, designed to be the key, turned out later to have been remarkably ineffective; and there is no reason to believe that Castro's air force, having survived the first and been dispersed into hiding, would have been knocked out by the second.
>
> The president's cancellation of the Monday morning air strike thus played only a minor role in the venture that came to so inglorious an end on Wednesday afternoon. It was already doomed long before Monday morning and he would have been far wiser, he told me later, if when the basic premises of the plan were already being shattered, he had cancelled the entire operation and not merely the second strike. For it was clear to him by then that he had in fact approved a plan having little resemblance to what he thought he had approved.

Sorensen says that he got all of his information from the president. "In the days that followed the fiasco," Sorensen says, "the president talked to me about it at length – in the mansion, in his office, and as we walked on the White House lawns. He was aghast at his own stupidity, angry at having been badly advised by some and let down by others." By the time Theodore Sorensen wrote his book, all the original air cover stories had unraveled. He gives simple descriptions of the reasons for the president's now admitted *cancellation* of the Monday mission against Castro's air bases.

When Arthur Schlesinger got around to writing *his* book, the stories about the weaknesses and execution of the plan by the CIA and military had also begun to unravel. Schlesinger, who was present at many of the meetings where decisions were made, says that President Kennedy was wracked by indecision as to whether to proceed or to cancel the operation he had inherited. Faced with the troublesome problem of what to do with the Cubans in Guatemala if he decided to cancel the invasion, he finally said: "If we have to get rid of these men, it is much better to dump them in Cuba than in the United States, if that is where they want to go."

Then, according to Schlesinger, President Kennedy cancelled the original plans prepared by the CIA and the Pentagon as "too spectacular" and insisted on one that he could be more comfortable with. "He did not want a big amphibious invasion," says Schlesinger. "He wanted a 'quiet' landing, preferably at night."

In all of the Bay of Pigs postmortems, the most compelling indictment of President Kennedy's bungling of the operation comes from the diary of one of Castro's pilots who participated in the action on the other side.

At dawn on Saturday, April 15, personnel at the air base at San Antonio de los Baños were awakened by an attack on the base by three of our brigade B-26s. One of the pilots on the base was Captain Jacques Lagas Navarro, an officer in Castro's Fuerza Aérea Rebelde (FAR), and second in command of a light bomb squadron equipped with B-26s.

Lagas was not a Cuban. He had come to Cuba from his native Chile in 1959 under contract to the FAR to instruct Cuban Air Force pilots on the B-26, and as an instructor of meteorology, navigation, and engineering. In addition to becoming a licensed pilot in Chile, Lagas had also served in the Chilean Marines for several years.

In late 1960 Lagas resigned his position as contract instructor pilot, was commissioned as a captain in the FAR, and appointed second in command of the B-26 squadron. His written reports of actions during the invasion at the Bay of Pigs, published in book form following his return to Chile, focus almost exclusively on the engagements of his own squadron and the personnel at San Antonio de los Baños. According to Captain Lagas, when the invading B-26s first appeared over the air base there was "terrible confusion and indecision" because the invading aircraft were painted exactly like the FAR's B-26s. They were not fired on until they opened fire themselves, resulting in an uncontested first pass by the invaders. The attack continued for 20 minutes and "quickly converted the base to a Hell."

At San Antonio de los Baños it was learned that simultaneous attacks had been made on the air bases at Libertad in Havana, and at Santiago on the southeast coast of Cuba. Lagas believed that four B-26s had made the raid on San Antonio de los Baños. (Actually, it was three.) Lagas learned of considerable damage and several aircraft destroyed at Libertad in Havana and he says that Captain Oreste Acosta died when his T-33 exploded in the air as he attempted to land at the field at Santiago. He does not say if Captain Acosta was shot down by enemy fire.

Saturday was spent cleaning up the air base and assessing damage. Lagas reports no flight from San Antonio de los Baños on that day. He does not say if combat air patrols were launched from either of the other two bases, but his description of the situation at his own base indicates that if the scheduled follow-up raid from Puerto Cabezas had been launched as planned on Saturday afternoon — even if only with another six or eight aircraft — the complete destruction of Castro's air force could have been accomplished.

Lagas says that Sunday was spent in complete inactivity. "All day long," he says, "the general staff kept absolute silence, as if nothing had happened, as if nothing was going to happen."

Everything was dark on the air base Sunday night. Most of the people spent the night in slit trenches. Lagas and his squadron commander, Captain Luis Silva, worked all night. They were able to get Lagas' personal plane and one other B-26 ready to fly. By five o'clock Monday morning the squadron had two serviceable aircraft and three pilots.

Lagas' B-26 was equipped with neither bombs nor a rear turret. It was armed with 50-calibre machine guns mounted in the nose. On his first mission to the Bay of Pigs on Monday morning, Lagas saw several ships, one of which had already been sunk. He also saw and identified two unmarked destroyers, flying no flags, cruising offshore. Because of his service at sea with the Chilean Marines, he was able to identify the class of these destroyers. He says that at that moment he wondered if the United States had declared war on Cuba.

Lagas attacked a ship unloading trucks and was met by a heavy barrage of machine-gun fire. He says that he also attacked and sank several small boats that were trying to get to shore with troops. Finishing up a pass at the boats, Lagas spotted a B-26 over Girón. There was no question in his mind that it was an enemy force B-26 because he was flying the FAR's only B-26 in the air at the moment.

Lagas positioned himself above and behind the invading B-26 which, according to him, was successfully and effectively strafing the road east of Girón. He closed to within 200 feet, tensely anticipating being fired upon by the enemy rear turret gunner. Lagas assumed that the invasion force aircraft were armed as were the B-26s of the FAR. As a matter of fact, the invasion force B-26s carried neither a rear turret gunner nor a bombardier.

Lagas says that the enemy B-26 started a left turn and for a brief instant he and the enemy pilot were looking at each other across a distance of less than 100 feet. Lagas fired a short burst which expended his remaining ammunition. He saw the impact of the few 50-calibre rounds against the left wing and engine nacelle of his adversary's aircraft. In the brief dogfight that followed, the invader fired two bursts at Lagas. The tracers passed forward under his wing. Lagas took violent evasive action. Coming around off the top of a steep, climbing turn, he spotted the enemy B-26 heading for the airfield at Girón, smoke pouring from the left engine. At that instant he heard the pilot of a T-33 come on the air. Lagas responded and described his position and the situation. The T-33 arrived over Girón as the crippled B-26 was making a final approach at Girón, gear and flaps down.

From behind the B-26 the T-33 pilot fired a short burst from his 50-calibre machine guns. The B-26 crashed on the field and burst into flames. Lagas assumed that all crew members were killed. Only the pilot was killed. The navigator was thrown clear of the aircraft and, miraculously, survived. Our C-46 that landed at Girón at daylight on Wednesday picked him up and flew him back to Puerto Cabezas.

Although this was the only enemy aircraft that Lagas saw on Monday morning, for some reason, he says, the FAR general staff believed that they were up against a superior air force. In his diary, Lagas specifically mentions the enemy air force as numbering 16 aircraft. At no time were there 16 of our aircraft over Cuba.

When Lagas returned to his base he learned that Captain Silva had been sent out on a mission in the other B-26 that had been returned to service. Silva suffered from ulcers so painful at times that he lost consciousness. He was on heavy medication, and his eyesight had been degenerating steadily for months. For many weeks Lagas had been urging the base commander to send Silva on extended leave for rest and recuperation. Lagas says that he was dumbfounded that Silva had been permitted to fly, and he became highly incensed when he learned that Silva's aircraft had been loaded with 500-pound bombs, but with no bomb sight and with an inexperienced cadet as bombadier.

"I felt a strange sensation," Lagas says. "Something told me that a secret and powerful force had taken hold of the FAR at this critical moment."

Without orders or instructions, Lagas ordered immediate refueling of his own aircraft and took off in pursuit of Silva who, by now, had a 30-minute head start. Since he was again without fighter escort, and his aircraft was unarmed, he flew a zigzag course down the beach, hugging the base of the clouds for protection against surprise attack. (Lagas was still unaware that he had little to fear from enemy aircraft.)

He heard Silva transmitting to base. Lagas picked up his own mike. "Grandfather, Grandfather," he called. "This is Skinny. Do not tell me your position. I repeat, do not tell me your position. I will find you."

"Roger, Skinny," Silva responded.

Lagas continued to search for Silva's B-26 and his escorting Sea Fury fighter flown by Lieutenant Gustova Bourzac. The two destroyers were still cruising offshore maintaining what Lagas estimated to be 25 to 30 knots. It was while observing the two destroyers that Lagas spotted Silva's B-26 cruising straight and level at 2,000 feet in the direction of the destroyers. Lagas did not know if Silva intended to try to bomb the two ships, but he did know that Silva would stand no chance against the antiaircraft cannon and rockets of the destroyers. At almost the same moment that he sighted Silva, Lagas says that he observed two faint lines of condensation pass close to his aircraft. He recognized these to be contrails from either cannon or rocket fire from one of the destroyers. As he was picking up his microphone to warn Silva away from the destroyers, Silva's aircraft disappeared in a tremendous explosion of flame and black smoke, destroyed by a direct hit from one of the ships' antiaircraft fire.

"Grandfather, Grandfather," Lagas called. "Come in Grandfather, this is Skinny."

"I don't know why I was calling," Lagas says. "I knew Silva was gone."

"Hey, bastard," a strange voice said over the radio, "why don't you ask your mother about your grandfather?"

"I knew the enemy was on our frequency," Lagas said. "We had not changed crystals in spite of the fact that I had solicited this a number of times from the general staff. I remained stunned. Mechanically I leveled off and headed for base. I spotted the Sea Fury that had supposedly escorted Silva. It was at altitude, losing itself in the clouds, headed north.

When he returned to base Lagas went to Operations to make a report. "With astonishment," he says, "I learned that Lieutenant Bourzac had reported sinking the destroyer that shot down Captain Silva, and that he had remained in the area until the ship sank to the bottom of the sea.

"I reproached him severely for his lack of honesty, manhood and professional honor. 'When did you sink it, coward?' I shouted. 'Go look at your airplane and you will see that it still has all the rockets.'

"Everyone headed for the Sea Fury and could see that, in fact, Bourzac had landed with all his rockets intact."

By four o'clock Tuesday morning mechanics working through the night had gotten three B-26s back in service, armed and ready to fly. However, the base commander, Captain Carreras, "retired" the squadron from service. He considered it too dangerous to fly aircraft painted identically like the enemy B-26s because antiaircraft forces were firing indiscriminately on any B-26 that came within range. This was quite true, according to Lagas. Later in the day, when the stand down had been rescinded, Lagas flew a one-airplane mission against a concentration of troops at a road intersection north of the Bay of Pigs. He says he made his bomb run through heavy Castro antiaircraft fire.

When he returned from this mission, Lagas found Captain Carreras waiting to accompany him on another mission, this time with a fighter escort of one Sea Fury and one T-33. After take-off, Lagas said, they circled the field for 40 minutes waiting for the escort which never arrived.

An electrical fire broke out in Lagas's plane from a short in the bomb circuitry. He landed to determine if repairs could be made. There was no wiring diagram and no electrical specialists available if there had been one. Captain Carreras continued to circle the field. Finally he landed and said that his machine guns would not fire. Lagas says that Captain Carreras was "carted off to jail" that night for cowardice.

Lagas was unaware of any air activity by our exile forces on Tuesday. We had dispatched six aircraft on Tuesday morning with minimal results. Lagas was under the impression that all enemy air activity had ceased.

By Wednesday morning Castro's entire complement of serviceable aircraft consisted of three B-26s with two qualified pilots, and two Sea Furys and two T-33s with eight pilots. Lagas flew two missions on Wednesday. On both missions he came under heavy attack from his own ground forces. The last mission was at five o'clock in the afternoon against a position in the city of Girón where the invaders were making a strong last stand.

Lagas was aware that U.S. Navy jets were operating in the area. He warned his turret gunner to watch for them, and also to be sure to distinguish between the Navy fighters and their own T-33s. On the final mission to Girón, Lagas's gunner said that he could not spot the T-33 that was supposed to be flying cover for them. Lagas said for him not to bother because he was "probably flying somewhere up around 30,000 feet."

Lagas says that his bombs hit the target in Girón, but on subsequent strafing runs he came under heavy machine-gun fire. His windshield was shot out and it was with difficulty that he made it back to San Antonio de los Baños to land. He learned that the Cuban Liberation Army had surrendered.

The celebration that followed featured Romeo and Juliet cigars and an abundance of champagne. Lieutenant Bourzac revived his story about sinking the destroyer. There was much loud talk, bragging, and "hangar flying." A Sea Fury pilot laughed loudly as he described how he had shot and killed an enemy pilot who had parachuted from his plane. (This was almost certainly not one of our B-26s. None would have been flying at sufficiently high altitude in any event. Lagas apparently believed del Pino, however.)

Lagas wrote that he tried unsuccessfully for a month to get in to see Defense Minister Raúl Castro (Fidel's brother). Finally, on June 19, 1961, he wrote a letter to the Minister Castro which was delivered to Che Guevara by a mutual girlfriend of Lagas and Guevara. In this letter, Lagas said: "Having exhausted all the normal ways to get to you, I have permitted myself to bother you by means of this present confidential informer."

Lagas detailed the following charges: (1) A pilot who was physically unfit to fly, and under medication, was ordered to fly a mission on Monday, April 17, in an aircraft that was not completely serviceable and not properly equipped for the mission. (2) Lagas refused an order of his superior to assign an unqualified pilot to fly a mission on Monday. (3) Although three B-26s were serviceable on Tuesday, the commander would not permit missions to be flown. (4) While he was sleeping, Lagas was robbed of his pistol and ammunition by pilots in his squadron. (5) Parents of a bombardier who had been killed had their automobile confiscated by a member of the political police force when they drove to San Antonio de los Baños to inquire about their son's death. (6) Captain Silva's car was confiscated by a political police officer instead of being delivered to Silva's wife after he was killed. (7) One of the pilots who had been jailed returned after two days to find that his money and personal effects had been stolen by a Captain and a Cadet in the squadron. (8) Lagas accused the pilot, del Pino, of war crimes and violation of the Geneva Conventions in the shooting of an enemy pilot who had parachuted from his crippled aircraft.

"The people to whom I refer have taken advantage of political influence and have practically taken over the FAR," Lagas wrote. "Because of all I have explained, I would appreciate it if you would order a full and complete investigation."

As Lagas said, "A letter like this could not go unanswered." It was not. But it was not what he expected. It was Lagas who was investigated. He was found "politically unreliable" and forced to resign his commission in the FAR. He was not jailed, but was kept under constant surveillance, and it was with great difficulty that he was able to "escape" (as he put it) from Cuba, and to return to his home in Chile. Lagas was killed in an accident shortly after publication of his diary.

Lagas was outspoken, controversial, and no doubt he made himself unpopular with his superiors. He was what would be known in most military organizations as a "popoff" (a kind of Cuban Leo Baker). But though he may have been naive, he was not stupid. He would not have made the charges in writing to Raúl Castro unless he believed that he could back them up. Where he went wrong was in his judgment of how Raúl Castro would respond.

Even discounted for exaggeration and the limited perspective of a squadron-level officer, the interesting thing about Lagas's diary is that it confirms not only the limited number and capability of Castro's aircraft at the time of the invasion, but also the poor quality of much of the leadership of the FAR at that time. (The cream of the FAR was in Czechoslovakia checking out on MIGs.)

And, for whatever else it may be worth, the Lagas account clearly confirms that we could have succeeded at the Bay of Pigs with even a small measure of additional effort and determination. It was a battle we could have won with any perseverance at all.

Trinidad

There are many reasons why the invasion of Cuba at the Bay of Pigs failed. None of these have anything to do with the operational plan as it was originally conceived; with the number or capability of the forces involved; with the arms and equipment with which these forces were supplied, or with the failure of insurgent forces inside Cuba to act.

Two things occurred that virtually ensured the failure of the mission to remove Fidel Castro from power. They were (1) the substitution of the Bay of Pigs for Trinidad as the invasion site, and (2) the sinking of two ships that carried arms, ammunition, and communications on Monday as the landing forces were going ashore.

Both of these circumstances were the direct result of decisions made by President Kennedy — not by the CIA, not by the Pentagon, not by anyone else.

Trinidad is a city of 20,000 inhabitants located on the southern coast of Cuba. It is 100 miles east of the Bay of Pigs, and about one-third the distance from the western tip of the island to the eastern end. Trinidad has a good harbor and airfield. The invasion of Cuba as it was originally planned by the CIA and approved by the Pentagon was to have been launched at Trinidad. However, the CIA was required by the White House to abandon the original operational plan only a few weeks before the invasion was actually launched on April 17, 1961.

From a tactical military point of view, one of Trinidad's distinguishing features is the adjacent terrain. To the east and northeast of Trinidad a small range of mountains rise to a height of 3,000 feet. To the west and northwest another range rises to a height of 4,000 feet. These are the Escambrays. There are no approaches through these hills from the north.

Access to Trinidad is by one main east-west highway, and a railroad from the east that terminates at Trinidad. Immediate objectives of the invaders force were the airfield; the port three miles south of the city; destruction of bridges on the access highway and the railroad, and occupation of the high ground north of the city by an airborne landing force. All the units of the invasion force would occupy a beachhead with a perimeter radius of one to three miles, inside which it would control the port, the airfield, the access road and railroad, the city itself, and the high ground to the northwest, north and northeast.

Reconnoitering outward from the beachhead for a distance of two to four miles would have linked the invaders with guerrilla forces operating in the mountains.

Additional tactical advantages recognized by the planners included Trinidad's remoteness from heavy concentrations of Castro military forces. There were sizable numbers of militia in the area but these troops had evidenced little hostility toward the guerrilla forces operating in the Escambrays. In fact, it was predictable that many of the militia would switch allegiance given any indication that the invasion effort could succeed.

Intelligence reports indicated that the civilian population was friendly. They had been lending support to the guerrillas in the hills. The ships transporting the invasion force would also carry 30,000 arms packs for both civilians and guerrillas. If things went badly in the initial stages, transition to a guerrilla mode was immediately possible by joining forces with the guerrillas already established only a few miles away in the Escambrays. If the invading force succeeded in establishing itself and eventually breaking out of the beachhead, there was the real possibility of severing Cuba in the middle, creating even graver problems for Castro. Trinidad would also have provided a suitable base for the immediate relocation of the government in exile, and its reconstitution as a revolutionary government in the homeland. *None* of these conditions obtained at the Bay of Pigs.

The Bay of Pigs site provided no port facilities with docks where equipment and supplies to support the expeditionary force could be unloaded. Approaches by sea to the beaches at the Bay of Pigs were studded with coral formations. Castro's military forces were only a short distance away with highway access to the area from three directions. Anticipated accretion of the expeditionary force was prevented by Castro's control of access roads and the population in the area of the beachhead. In fact there *was* no beachhead in the sense that the invading force occupied and controlled a specific area within a well-defined perimeter. Rather, there were "lodgements" of force elements at three separate places on the beach over a distance of 30 miles.

The surrounding Zapata swamps were inhospitable and poorly suited to guerrilla activities requiring support and resupply from the outside. There was little hope for escape from the Bay of Pigs if things went wrong. The Escambray Mountains where there were guerrilla forces already in place were a hundred miles distant.

The sole reason for abandoning the carefully planned operation at Trinidad was President Kennedy's perception that the Trinidad operation was too "spectacular." He directed the CIA planners to come up with an alternate plan to employ the exile Cuban forces. To be acceptable to the president, this plan had to provide for a "quiet" landing, preferably at night, that would not have the appearance of a "World War II assault." What he wanted was an operation in which United States participation could be credibly denied in order to avoid adverse reactions by Latin American nations and our other allies; possible expulsion from the Organization of American States, and censure by the United Nations.

In President Kennedy's mind, it was necessary that air strikes against Cuban targets be perceived as having been launched from within Cuba in order to preserve the fiction that these attacks were being made by rebelling pilots in Castro's own air force. And it was not only the mere perception that President Kennedy insisted on. He also insisted that the raids must in actual fact be launched from an airfield in Cuba that had already been taken and secured by the invading Cuban expeditionary force.

The selection at the Bay of Pigs was made only after exhaustive reconnaissance. Subsequent allegations that the Joint Chiefs of Staff had "approved" the Zapata operation are not true. At a hearing before the Taylor investigating committee, Chairman of the JCS, General Lyman Lemnitzer made this clear.

> I don't know how much Secretary (of State) Rusk or any of his other people were involved. As a matter of fact, it was a disappointment to me because I thought we had a plan that had been thoroughly worked out and I hated to see another delay and another complete evaluation of the island. It caused some concern both in my group and in the CIA. Mr. Mann (Assistant Secretary of State) liked the Zapata plan because it provided us with plausible denial. I indicated that the JCS had gone over the alternatives and didn't think any of them were as good as the original Trinidad plan. Then I said this, that it was not clear to me why Zapata was any more acceptable from the political point of view than the Trinidad plan. Whereupon Mr. Mann replied that it gave plausible denial to the launching of air operations from outside Cuba. He said we needed a facade behind which we could deny that these attacks came out of the United States, Guatemala or Nicaragua.

In additional testimony before the investigating committee General Lemnitzer reiterated that with respect to the Zapata plan, the Joint Chiefs did no more than make a choice from three alternatives to the Trinidad plan.

> *Statement:* You mention the preference for Trinidad — I'm not sure whether you're aware of it, but the Secretary of Defense apparently never appreciated that point. In fact, he had the impression that the Chiefs thought that Zapata was the better of the two plans.
> *General Lemnitzer:* I just don't understand how he got that impression. I can show you in my notes on two accounts where I called it to his

attention. We also put in writing that "of the alternate plans, alternative three is considered the most feasible and likely to accomplish the objectives of the present paramilitary plan." I don't see how you can say it any clearer than that.

In his insistence on a "quiet" landing, President Kennedy also caused a substantial revision in the air operations that were critical to the success of the invasion — no matter where the troops went ashore.

The primary mission of the expeditionary air force was to destroy the FAR on the ground. This was to have been accomplished in the original operation by an all-out raid at dawn on D-day against three air force bases where reconnaissance photos had located all of Castro's combat aircraft. A maximum effort strike on D-day could, and was planned to, launch 21 B-26s against these three targets. On D-day in Puerto Cabezas we had 21 B-26s and 25 B-26 pilots — 17 Cubans and eight Americans if you count Riley Shamburger and Hal McGee. Instead, only eight of our aircraft were launched against Castro's three air bases — and not on D-day but on D-2 (Saturday, two days before D-day).

The result was that not all of Castro's aircraft were destroyed, although the surprise was complete. Castro was left with two single-engine Sea Fury fighters, two T-33s (armed), and three B-26s. This was not a bad job considering the limited number of aircraft that had been involved in our attack.

The Saturday morning raid put Castro on notice that the long-anticipated invasion was imminent, although he had no way of knowing that it would be two full days before any armed forces hit the beach. In the two day lull, Castro's army, militia and police forces fanned out across the island. They rounded up and imprisoned tens of thousands of committed and potential dissidents who could have, and probably would have, swelled the ranks of the expeditionary forces once it was established ashore. Prior to an invasion that showed some signs of success, there was no way that Cubans who may have wanted to, could defect. There was no place and nothing for them to defect *to.*

The D-2 air raid was *not* a part of the original plan of operation. It was designed purely for the political purposes perceived by President Kennedy to be necessary. It was planned to coincide with the landing of the B-26 piloted by Captain Zúñiga in Miami in an incredibly ill-conceived attempt to provide evidence of a rebellion of Castro air force pilots in Cuba. The scheme and the story that went with it were tissue thin. There was no way it could hold up for more than a few hours; just long enough for the media to determine that Zúñiga's aircraft was configured entirely differently from Castro's B-26s. Zúñiga's B-26 had no tail turret guns; Castro's did. Zúñiga's B-26 had six 50-calibre machine guns mounted in a metal nose cone; Castro's B-26s had plastic nose cones and guns mounted in the wings.

Robert Kennedy said at this time that the president's decisions were dictated by Zúñiga's cover story falling apart, and by the "surfacing" of the role of the United States. The role of the United States government had surfaced long before April 17, 1961. What was falling apart was the entire mission itself under the pressure of White House policy and operational decisions that left no chance for the mission's successful accomplishment.

As indicated in their testimony before the Taylor Committee, the Joint Chiefs of Staff accepted the Zapata swamps site at the Bay of Pigs only as the best of three alternatives to Trinidad. To the CIA and the military, Zapata represented *only* a change in the landing site. The air mission remained unchanged — massive, simultaneous, surprise attacks against critical targets to maintain control of the air. This was an entirely obtainable objective, even at the Bay of Pigs. Under no circumstances would the military or the CIA have made a favorable assessment of a plan that did not include D-day air strikes — not at Trinidad, not at Zapata, not anywhere.

In testimony before the Taylor Committee, Commandant of the Marine Corps, General David M. Shoup, made these remarks:

> I don't know what happened at a lot of meetings at the White House or the State Department, but I do know this, that within the corporate body, I, for one, emphasized time after time that we had to have air superiority, and we had to have help to fend off the force they were going to have opposing them down there.
>
> I want to tell you this right now. Had I, as an individual, heard that they were going to call off the air strikes, I'd have asked that the Commander-in-Chief be informed. I'd have called him myself because it was absolutely essential to success. The D-2 affair was only a half effort.

General Shoup's outrage is understandable, but he was not aware that it was the Commander-in-Chief himself who cancelled the D-day strikes.

In response to General Shoup's remarks, CIA Director Allen Dulles said, "General, may I add this: The D-2 day was essentially a plot, not a plan." Further testimony by General Lemnitzer included the following exchange with General Maxwell Taylor:

> *General Taylor:* What led to the idea that it was necessary to maintain that all of the air strikes emanated from Cuba?
> *General Lemnitzer:* We were strong for the Trinidad plan. However, about the middle of March during a meeting at the White House, Mr. Mann was gravely concerned about the impact throughout Latin America of these air strikes coming from outside Cuba. He hammered at the point repeatedly and wanted to know if there wasn't some area in Cuba where they could land on a ready made area. At the conclusion of the meeting,

CIA was directed to review the whole idea and come up with alternative landing areas other than Trinidad to provide plausibility to the story that the aircraft had come from within Cuba.

General Taylor: When you commented on Zapata the first time, the air plan was for D-day strikes only, but with no limitations.

General Lemnitzer: That's correct.

General Taylor: Later there were limited strikes on D-2 and limited strikes on D-day. Would you comment on this watering down of the air plan? Were the chiefs satisfied with this?

General Lemnitzer: The D-2 strikes were added for nonmilitary reasons. We would have preferred to do without the D-2 strikes. They were never intended to accomplish the destruction of the Castro air force. They were to lend plausibility to the story that the strikes had been launched from within Cuba.

When General Lemnitzer learned of the cancellation of the D-Day air strikes it was two o'clock in the morning. The attack at the Bay of Pigs was launched at dawn.

Some of the heaviest criticism directed at the CIA by journalists, academics, many of the Cuban people, and other not-well-qualified Monday morning quarterbacks focused on the failure to keep guerrilla forces and dissidents inside Cuba informed of the plans and dates for the invasion.

Typical of many of the attacks on the CIA for the way it handled this aspect of the plan, is an analysis made by Luis E. Arguilar, a professor of history at Georgetown University.

"First consider the organizer's (CIA) assumption that ultimate success will depend upon political factors, i.e., a sizable popular uprising," says Arguilar. "This was a correct evaluation. Without the active support of important sectors of the Cuban population, the small landing force had no chance of success."

Professor Arguilar is correct. Popular support was always recognized, and counted on, as a key element in the success of the overall operation. Accordingly, 30,000 weapons packs to supply anti–Castro Cubans were on board one of the ships sunk first thing Monday morning at the Bay of Pigs. As important as an "uprising" may have been, even more important was the matter of timing for any such activity.

"With the pretext of secrecy" (pretext?), Arguilar continues, "no clear explanation of the expedition's objectives was given to the Cuban people. Left in the dark about what was happening, anti–Castro elements were supposed to risk their lives for an operation of which they knew nothing."

The point is, they were *not* supposed to risk their lives unnecessarily.

"To make matters worse," Professor Arguilar says, "the pretense of secrecy had not fooled Castro. Four days before the invasion, before they had learned what was happening, Castro's suspected opponents were arrested by the thousands. Nevertheless, the failure of the expected uprising was blamed on the Cubans." (Who blamed the Cubans?)

Professor Arguilar has made a serious misstatement of fact. It is not a simple, inconsequential error of a couple of days between one event and another. It creates an entirely false and misleading perception of cause and effect. The arrests which occurred were *two* days before the invasion, not four, and they were triggered by the D-2 air raid on Saturday morning. This was a strike which was *not* planned by the CIA and the military. It was superimposed by President Kennedy himself as part of a public relations scheme that was seriously flawed.

Teaching history is not hard, I guess, if you get to write it yourself, but the question of what the Cubans knew, and when they knew it, deserves much more thoughtful treatment than it has received at the hands and from the pen of Professor Arguilar and others.

At a hearing before the Senate Foreign Relations Committee on May 2, 1961, CIA Director Allen Dulles testified on this subject:

> I want to correct what may be slight misapprehension. We did not count on — one might hope for it, but we did not count on — any immediate uprising in Cuba. Some people have said, "Well, there was a great mistake in intelligence because there wasn't an immediate uprising."
>
> If a beachhead had been held, we did expect, and I think this was borne out by some facts we will bring out later, that there would be substantial accretions to any force that did establish a beachhead.
>
> During World War II I worked very closely in Switzerland with the French underground. Anyone, I think, who has worked with an underground realizes that the worst thing one can do is to precipitate an early uprising of an underground. We had great difficulty keeping the French down during the period prior to the landings and before the beachhead in Normandy was established.
>
> There has been some criticism in the press, I note, that the underground was not alerted to this particular operation. That was very carefully planned. In the first place, if you had alerted the underground to the operation, everybody would have known it. In the second place, if you alerted them to rise up before they had the arms and equipment to give a good account of themselves, it would just have been a slaughter.
>
> So all the business in the press that the intelligence was wrong, that there was no great uprising — we had neither tried to have an uprising at the time of the landing, nor had we prepared them for it, nor told them about it. There could not have been any uprising any more on that day than any other day.
>
> Now, if there had been a beachhead established, we do not know what effect that might have had. But we would have hoped that initially there would not have been an uprising, but that there would have been accretions and a buildup of the underground until the time came, as in the case of the liberation of France.

Following the failure of the invasion at the Bay of Pigs, judgments were made and opinions formed in the public's mind on the basis of stories and reports by journalists and historians who were poorly informed because

because they were, in some cases, the unwitting victims of an organized effort to shift responsibility for this failure to the undeserving shoulders of the CIA and the Pentagon.

The CIA has not yet fully recovered from this blow, and the United States will be a long time recovering from the loss of confidence and credibility it suffered at the Bay of Pigs in the eyes of the world.

Conclusion

The Bay of Pigs is one of the most controversial episodes in the history of United States foreign affairs. The consequences of this failed effort to depose Fidel Castro are far reaching and may not yet have been fully measured. Worldwide the prestige of the United States government suffered a blow from which it has not fully recovered. One of the consequences of our failure to remove Castro from power in Cuba is that an armed garrison of a Marxist dictatorship remains in place only 90 miles off the coast of Florida. Cuba today is a platform from which efforts to subvert democratic governments can be launched throughout our hemisphere. Today El Salvador, Honduras, and Guatemala are threatened. Nicaragua has already fallen. Our failure to remove Castro in 1961 returns to haunt us today.

In addressing this threat we seem to be handicapped by built-in flaws in the machinery and operation of our government. One of these is an inability to formulate and implement consistent foreign policies to establish and maintain long-range goals. No better example exists than the affair at the Bay of Pigs.

In December 1960 the United States government became engaged in an effort to remove a government from the island of Cuba which we perceived to be a threat to the security of our nation. One month later in January 1961, a new president and a new administration of government, with new and different foreign policies and goals, performed radical surgery on the plans of the previous administration. This resulted in a debacle that destroyed the credibility of the United States and the effectiveness of the Central Intelligence Agency, an agency of government that occupies a point position in our continuing struggle for human rights.

Following the fiasco at the Bay of Pigs, efforts were made to explain the event as a failure of the CIA. That these efforts were successful is evident. Today "Bay of Pigs" has become an almost generic term, synonymous with "CIA bungling." Understandably, the CIA has not been able to go public in its own defense. But the record should be made clear, not only in the interest of historical accuracy, but also as a frightening demonstration of the power of people in very high places of authority and command to avoid the consequences of their own actions — if they should be so disposed. The record is clear:

It was not the CIA that cancelled air attacks vital to the success of the mission.

It was not the CIA that insisted on a "quiet" landing, "preferably at night" or that changed the invasion site from Trinidad to the Bay of Pigs and the surrounding Zapata swamps, and who cut down the strength of attacks against Castro's air bases.

It was not the CIA that said ". . . if we have to get rid of these men it is much better to dump them in Cuba. . . ."

It was not the CIA that sent the Cuban freedom fighters ashore unprotected against Castro's combat aircraft.

And it was not the CIA that deceived the American people about how and why this operation went wrong.

The CIA is an agency of the United States government that operates behind closed doors. It is an agency whose books are not open to general public inspection. Certainly a part of its stock-in-trade is deception and subversion. And its activities sometimes appear to be in conflict with our government's expressed policies, and are, sometimes, the antithesis of our own popular concepts of what America is supposed to stand for in the eyes of the rest of the world.

This is an issue that deeply troubles many Americans. We want to believe in the principles expressed in our Constitution and in our Declaration of Independence. We want to believe that we are sincere in what we say about defending the rights of self-determination for the people of all nations, and we want to believe that America stands by and supports the principles expressed in the Charters of the United Nations and of the Organization of American States.

In the emotional confusion created by an affair like the Bay of Pigs (or Chile, or Iran), immediate public reaction is often to single out for censure the government agency most intimately involved, i.e., the CIA. This is understandable but unfortunate, for while it is by no means above reproach, the intelligence community does not function independently. It is not a rogue elephant rampaging out of control. It does, or attempts to do, what it is told. The Bay of Pigs was not some kind of CIA caper. It was a covert operation of the United States government. It was also the kind of adventure that once launched should *never* have been allowed to fail.

We are faced with these questions: Is there ever a justification for the United States government to organize and support a covert effort to depose by armed force the head of government of another independent nation, or under any circumstances, and by any means, covert or otherwise, to interfere in the internal affairs of another state?

And is there ever a justification for the government to withhold information and to deceive the people of the United States of the fact that it may be engaged in such activities? (In plainer language, does the government have the right to lie?)

Arthur Sylvester, a former Assistant Secretary of the Defense, said that the government has an inherent right to lie to protect its people. He told the story of the "lying Baptists" to make his point.

According to this story, back in 1804 Baptists became divided into two camps over an issue involving a right to lie under certain circumstances. The question posed was whether a man with three children captured by a band of savage Indians, had the right to lie to protect the life of a fourth child who was hidden from the savages. The "lying Baptists" said yes. The "truthful Baptists" said no.

Baptists and Indians aside, most people will agree that an essential duty and responsibility of government is to ensure the peace and security of the nation and its citizens. If it is able, a government should maintain a military establishment strong enough to defeat an enemy in armed conflict, or, better still, to deter an enemy from starting a conflict in the first place. In a condition of "declared" war — hot, that is, instead of cold — few will argue with the right, even the duty, of the government to maintain the tightest security over secret codes, intelligence activities, and covert operations. No more than we would condemn the father who saved his child from the marauding Indians by "lying," would we condemn our government for "lying" to save us.

Most people would line up on the side of the father who lied to save his child. And probably most people would line up on the side of the government when it uses a "Top Secret" stamp to conceal its activities from a self-declared enemy. The trouble is, the same "Top Secret" stamp too often is used to protect people in high places from having to suffer the consequences of their failures. This is not lying to protect the child. This is lying to protect the father. Given the facts, most people would have no difficulty making the distinction.

Perhaps what it all comes down to on the bottom line is this: It is important that we should be strong enough to win a World War III — if it comes to that. More important than winning World War III is preventing World War III. Therefore, whatever means we would accept to win World War III, should we not as readily accept to prevent it?

Postscript

One of the most frustrating aspects of the work of an investigative journalist is probably encountered when he sets out to investigate activities of one or another of the agencies that make up the government's "intelligence community." Nowhere else will he find more impenetrable stone walls erected to prevent him from doing his job. The very nature of intelligence activities imposes an inflexible requirement for secrecy. The job of the investigative journalist, on the other hand, is to "investigate" and to make public the results of his efforts. In the adversarial relationship which inevitably develops, the intelligence agency may become the "enemy." This may explain in part why the Central Intelligence Agency, for instance, suffers from an almost univerally bad press.

In his frustration the journalist may tend to see the barriers erected against him, not as barriers erected to protect the security interests of the nation, but as barriers erected to protect the agency from exposing to the outside world its misconduct and malfeasance. In these circumstances it is understandable if objectivity sometimes suffers. (In the opening paragraphs of his book, Peter Wyden lets us know right up front where he is going. He describes the CIA as ". . . a government agency routinely, daily committing unconstitutional acts against its own citizens in its own country." He also headlines two pages of photographs of intelligence and military officers as "The CIA Plotters.")

Although their sources are routinely decribed as "unimpeachable" — and the authors may have no reason to believe otherwise — the information these high level sources provide is often highly inaccurate, sometimes, perhaps, even deliberately deceptive. And sometimes it is not even credible. (A B-26, for instance, cannot cruise around over Cuba for two-and-one-half hours before heading back to Nicaragua which is another three hours' distance across the Caribbean Sea.) Actions are described that never took place, with results that never occurred. Conversations are quoted verbatim that the authors could not possibly have heard.

David Wise, Haynes Johnson, Mario Lazo and Peter Wyden, among others, have written lengthy accounts describing the operation at the Bay of Pigs in great and highly dramatic detail. Unquestionably they are experienced, hard-working, competent journalists. But if each were to read the book of the others, all might be hard put to recognize that they describe the same events.

How historians will deal with the contradictions in these chronicles, and with those who were the sources of information on which they are based, remains to be seen.

Appendix A: Personnel

Birmingham Contingent

Major General Reid Doster
Lieutenant Colonel Joseph L. Shannon (Hal McGee)
Major Riley Shamburger

Doster, Shannon, and Shamburger were at a higher level in the chain of command than the airmen who were recruited to fly support missions for the Cubans. They were responsible not only for the American and Cuban pilots, but also for organizing and supervising the large contingent of specialists required to support an air operation in the field. Most, but not all, of the echelon of ground support specialists came from the 117th Tactical Reconnaissance Wing of the Alabama Air Guard commanded by General Doster in Birmingham.

B-26 Pilots

Don Gordon, Bill Peterson, Al Walters, Joe Hinkle, Pete Ray, Ron Smith

C-54 Pilots

Ernie King, Gordon Neilson, Fred Ealey, Phil Chapman, Buck Persons, Earl Carter (discharged from project)

Flight Engineers

Sandy Sanders, Red Cornish, Leo Baker

Radio Operators

Jack Vernon, Wade Gray

Company (CIA) Personnel

Birmingham Briefers and Contract Negotiators

Al, Jake, Frank, Hoyt

Company Personnel in Florida

Eric, Mac (operational training), Jim, Les, Ferd "Magellan" Dutton, Nick

Company Commanders in Central America

Larry, Al, Frank, Vic and Connie (two company pilots), Burt

A Note on the Names

Except for Doster, Shamburger, Shannon, Ray, Gray and Baker, all of these names are fictitious. They are not even the "phonies" assigned to them by the company. In some cases their home states and civilian backgrounds are fictitious. The reason for this is that following their participation in the operation at the Bay of Pigs, I would have no way of knowing what continuing activities for the company, if any, these people may have engaged in, or what the consequences for some might be for connecting them, even now, with the Bay of Pigs. Knowing who everyone is, or was, adds nothing to the story. Even if knowing their true identities would no longer make any difference, it is each individual's prerogative to make known his role if he so chooses. (Some have. Some have not.) None of these people, however, are fictitious characters.

The participation of General Doster was revealed by an Air Force general officer in an interview with Chicago's *American*. The names of the four men who lost their lives at the Bay of Pigs were revealed in cover stories created to account for their presence in Central America. Colonel Shannon's role has been documented more recently by journalists who have written their own accounts of the event. When I began to write this story I chose the name "Hal McGee" for Colonel Shannon. I have continued to use it throughout.

Appendix B: Chronology

1948 Beginning of the "Cold War." The Organization of American States met in Rio de Janeiro. United States Latin American policy was established with an aim to "defend" Western Hemisphere against communist threats.

1954 Expedition of Guatemalan exiles armed and supported by the U.S. government invaded Guatemala and toppled the leftist government of Juan Jacobo Arbenz.

1959 The dictator Fulgencio Batista fled Cuba and Fidel Castro made his triumphant entry into Havana. Castro's increasingly authoritarian control of government, mass executions of opponents, and growing communist influence were resisted by many Cubans, including influential figures in his "26th of July" movement. Relations between the Castro government and the United States deteriorated rapidly.

January 3, 1960 Eisenhower administration severed diplomatic relations with Cuba.

January–April 1960 By early 1960, plans to depose Castro had begun to evolve.

March 17, 1960 President Eisenhower approved program of covert action against Castro government.

May 1960 Thompson-Cornwall, Inc., began construction of an air base at Retalhuleu, Guatemala, on property owned by Roberto Alejo, brother of the Guatemalan ambassador to the United States.

May 17, 1960 "Radio Swan," operated by the U.S. government on Swan Island in the Caribbean, began regular broadcasts directed primarily at a Cuban audience.

June–November 1960 Declining confidence in the effectiveness of a purely guerrilla operation resulted in the adoption of a concept of a Cuban strike force supported by a small tactical air force. Emphasis was redirected toward training of this assault force and the "Liberation Air Force."

November 29, 1960 President Eisenhower was briefed on the new paramilitary concept. He indicated that he wished the project expedited. During this period detailed planning was initiated for the assault on Trinidad.

January 28, 1961 President Kennedy received first briefing on developing plans.

February–May 1961   During this period the American air crews contracted with the CIA to fly support missions for the Cuban invasion force. The B-26 pilots proceeded to Miami and then to Retalhuleu where they provided intensive operational training for the Cuban air crews. After a short period of recurrent operational training in Florida, the C-54 pilots flew to Retalhuleu where they were employed in flying equipment, supplies, arms and ammunition from Retalhuleu to Puerto Cabezas in Nicaragua. In April the C-54 pilots transported the entire Cuban invasion force from its training base in Guatemala to the staging base and transport ships at Puerto Cabezas.

March 11, 1961   President Kennedy ordered an alternative to Trinidad for employing the Cuban forces that would provide for a "quiet" landing, preferably at night, avoiding the appearance of a "World War II assault."

March 14, 1961   Three alternatives were presented to the Joint Chiefs of Staff. The Joint Chiefs reported that of the three, the Zapata alternative was the best, adding that none of the alternatives were considered as feasible and likely to accomplish the objective as the Trinidad plan. What the Joint Chiefs were approving was an alternative site, not major changes in an operational plan which included full-scale strikes against Cuba's air bases on D-day in order to gain full control of the air.

April 15, 1961 (two days before D-day)   Eight B-26s were launched against Castro air bases. Three aircraft attacked Campo Libertad, three attacked San Antonio de los Baños, and two aircraft attacked the base at Santiago. No follow-up attacks were launched. This limited effort left Castro with six to eight aircraft which were, or could be made, operational.

April 16, 1961 (one day before D-day)   Planned air strike against massed forces of Castro's artillery, armored and mobile equipment was cancelled.

April 17, 1961 (D-day)   Invasion force landed before daylight on the beaches at Girón and on the western shore of the Bay of Pigs. No beachhead with a well-defined perimeter was ever established. Last minute cancellation of D-day attacks that were to complete the destruction of Castro's air force made possible the sinking of the *Houston* and *Río Escondido*. These ships carried ammunition resupply and communications equipment.

April 18, 1961 (one day after D-day)   Six B-26s were launched after midnight. Bad weather and low visibility prevented identification of targets.

April 19, 1961 (two days after D-day)   Assault forces, their ammunition exhausted, were pushed back down the roads from the north and northwest onto the beach at Girón and into the swamps on the Zapata peninsula. Some men were able to escape out to sea and onto small offshore islands where they were picked up by the U.S. Navy and commercial ships. Approximately 1,000 of the assault forces were captured and imprisoned. A final mission was launched early in the morning of Wednesday, April 19. Five B-26s were crewed by ten Americans. A sixth B-26 was flown by Gonzalo Herrera. Two of the aircraft with four Americans were shot down. By five o'clock Wednesday afternoon, April 19, all resistance had ended.

Index